The Day that Time Stood Still

Mike Gomm

Copyright © 2022 Mike Gomm
All rights reserved.
ISBN: 9798355911683

DEDICATION

This book is dedicated to all our family and friends who stood with us in pray during this difficult time.

Acknowledgements

All bible references are taken from the New King James version of the bible.

FOREWORD

Pearl Angela Coleman, City of God Ministries.

This book is an incredible, painstaking documentary of a day by day, and almost hour by hour witness of the mercy of Christ for a beloved born-again Christian husband who was, with his two heroic sons aged 13 and 15 years, standing steadfast together for the life of a Christian mother and wife.

The book spoke to me strongly of the Christian upbringing of those two young lads who found their mother on her bedroom floor, clearly unconscious for some eight hours with a truly massive brain haemorrhage. It is deeply moving to see how they coped with such a terrifying situation. God bless them!

This incredible record not only deals with the extraordinary timing of the Lord's provision almost minute by minute, reading the book also searched my heart.

I know well as a medical journalist, the provision of the John Radcliffe Hospital at Oxford really are second to none.

Interlaced with scriptures, the book illustrates total dependence on the mercy of the Lord. The faith of Helen's dear family could move mountains in spite of the extreme seriousness of a complicated massive brain bleed.

Helen had first been ambulanced to the Royal Berkshire Hospital when it was immediately observed how very serious her condition was. Seen at the Neuro Intensive Care Unit at the John Radcliffe it became very clear that urgent immediate tracheotomy and all manner of tubes and ventilators were needed as well as surgery.

The consultant, who was not supposed to be on duty that day, later told Mike that when he opened her skull, the bleed was so huge, that he expected her brain to slide out!

The book documents the travelling nightmare of back and forth, with two young boys missing school some days, and is alive with details of changes that needed to be made in all their lives, and the outstanding kindness of hospital staff and the incredible support of their church and prayer warriors across the world.

The book took me three and a half hours to read in bed when I felt very ill and distressed, but I could not put it down because of the inspiration it gave me to keep standing on The Word.

Psalm 103 came to mind which emphasises that He sent His Word to deliver us from destruction. Helen's precious testimony on CD illustrates that Helen's memory of scripture prevailed in her darkest hour and that it can do so for every believer who knows their Bible.

I pray that this book, which glorifies the Lord and illustrates for me the safety of a family and a loving supportive fellowship united by Christ, will open the eyes of the reader and be a comfort to those in need as it was for me.

Introduction

The consultant sat us down in his office and said, "You have a better chance of winning the lottery than of having the recovery I see before me now" Perhaps this was his way of saying this is a miracle.

How did we get to this point? What happened?

I will recount to you the miracles and events that unfolded for us, an ordinary family, but a family who believed in God and the salvation brought about by the death and resurrection of Jesus Christ. 'Why us?' is not a question to be asked. We had to respond as Mary, the mother of Jesus, responded: "How can this be?", when she discovered she was carrying the son of God.

In this account I have chosen not to name people, but if they wish to write their own account of events then they are free to do so. I have deliberately not named the medical staff as that certainly would not be right.

We continue to be amazed at the people God brought to the right place at the right time and the way circumstances and situations changed as a result of prayer. We are truly grateful to the friends and family who are also medical professionals without whose input and guidance we would not have survived so easily. What became obvious as time went on, is that so many people were a piece of the jigsaw that came together so well.

We still do not understand why certain things did happen and why others did not, but I guess those are questions for heaven and we may never know the answers. A few people over the months were true angels of God to us as a family and showed a real servant heart.

It is my desire that as you read this, you reflect on your own life and what God has for you and that what we have been through might bring you closer to God and that you fulfil His purposes in your life.

The text will be narrative, but certain things will be revisited as information came to us retrospectively. As I write each day's events the beginning, will be part of the email I sent out daily to friends and family so they could pray informatively and for those prayers we are truly thankful to God. These emails may appear to contain repetition of the narrative text, but they are the summary sent out on a daily basis so that people could pray.

Firstly some background about ourselves.

Helen and I were married in 1986 in the Church we attend and that I had joined in September 1983. We have two sons who themselves are miracle babies (that is another story). They were born in 1996 and 1998 and were 15 and 13 respectively at the time of their mother's collapse. I work in a large secondary comprehensive school and at the time was one of the Elders in the Church. Helen worked as part of the Church Administration team and she was effectively the team leader.

Chapter 1
A very long day –
(Friday 10th February 2012)

The day had started early – I had been woken by Helen around 5.00am with her complaining about having a very bad migraine-type headache and feeling a bit sick. She had felt that way the day before, but after we had all left for school, she went back to bed, and her head had cleared. We had all been working very hard and this was the last day before the half term holiday. We were all looking for some rest and relaxation over the week ahead. It had been snowing overnight and there was about an inch of snow on the drive. I went back to sleep and was woken by the alarm about 6.10am. I dozed for a few minutes and the alarm clocks round the house reminded us all that it was a school day and the time was now 6.20am.

Helen was still complaining about her head, but we prayed as usual to commit the day into God's hands and then I got up to get washed and dressed whilst Helen went downstairs to make the tea and start the lunch boxes for our children. They were quite excited about the snow, and I remember them talking about a decent snowball fight at school. I just wished the snow, had come a day later as I anticipated the hill out of the village could be slippery, as could the lanes out to school. I made my lunch and breakfast and was soon out of the door. Once I was onto the main road, the snow had only settled on the edges of the road as the gritting lorries had done a good job and my journey to school was not much longer than usual.

I am a secondary Physics and Information and Communications Technology teacher with responsibilities for helping with the delivery of ICT in the classroom along with assisting and supporting staff with ICT 'how to' issues. The school has 1800 students, and I am a tutor in the sixth form.

I was one of the first to arrive in our area and I had to put the water heater on for a cuppa as nobody else had arrived yet. This heated up while my laptop booted up and I logged onto the network. I duly made myself a cup of tea and then I rang Helen to give her a 'personal road report' and she said she was going back to bed as her head was really bad and she felt sick. Her only major task of the day was to produce the weekly Sunday newsletter for the Church and so I said that if she needed to take the day off I would nip into the Church office on my way home and collect the bits to do the newsletter at home that evening. I told her I loved her and that I would see her later and was looking forward to the half term break. She said she would ring our pastor and tell him that she was feeling unwell and would be late in. She never got to make that telephone call.

That was the last rational conversation I was to have with Helen for several weeks. I then got stuck into my day. I later discovered that she had seen the boys off to school and had then made a fresh cup of tea which she had not drunk, which was most unusual for her. She had taken some pictures of the snow on her digital camera from the front door about 8.05am and then she had put the camera down and gone upstairs. Unusually, she had not put the camera back where it lives.

My classes seemed to both drag and fly past as I kept looking at my email to see if there was one from Helen to say she was at work and feeling better, or one from home telling me how she was.

I was not teaching the last lesson on that Friday, so I sorted things out for after half-term and I had the strangest vision of Timothy and Stephen coming home and finding their mother dead in the bed. I dismissed it from my mind as a silly thought and a distraction from the enemy. I then wrote a 'to do' list in my diary for the holiday and a 'to do' list for the Monday after half-term. I went and had a conversation with the ICT support team and to wish them a good break and then I registered my Year12 tutor group at the end of the day.

I left promptly as I wanted to get the stuff from the Church for the newsletter and go home. We were due at my parents' house, the other side of London, the next day and so I pulled into the petrol station to fill up the tank on the people carrier. My mobile rang, but I did not get it out of my pocket in time to get the call, and it was a missed call from my youngest son. I assumed that he wanted to go out in the snow on his bike, so I went to pay for the fuel, but the missed call troubled me, so I tried to ring the home landline but this was engaged and so I tried my son on his mobile.

He was crying on the other end of the phone to say that they had come home and found that mum had collapsed on the floor and that Tim had called for an ambulance and was keeping her alive whilst waiting. I told him I was on my way and that I would be there as soon as I could. I then rang our Pastor to tell him what had happened. I did not care if the police caught me using the phone whilst driving and I drove as fast as possible home whilst praying for God to keep Helen alive. How could a journey be so long? I was so glad I knew the road really well, particularly in those snowy conditions.

I arrived home to find the emergency response car outside our house and ran upstairs to find the paramedic attending to Helen on the bedroom floor and two upset children on the landing. Our Pastor followed me through the door and he then started ringing people.

How long can an ambulance take to arrive? The paramedic told me to pack some provisions as they would be taking Helen to the Royal Berkshire Hospital (RBH) and that we could be there some time. Our son Stephen had given the paramedic all of Helen's drugs. Helen was on oxygen and the paramedic had her connected to a heart monitor and she was on the floor very agitated and trying to move around, but was unable to control any of her movements. As we were to discover later this was due to brain distress.

Eventually, the ambulance arrived 40 minutes after the first call and they seemed to take forever to get Helen into the ambulance and our son Tim went with Helen so that I could communicate with him at her side. Stephen packed a rucksack with crisps, chocolate biscuits and bottles of squash. He also grabbed his purse of money as he was the only one with any cash. We locked the house and left for the Royal Berkshire Hospital (RBH), not knowing when we would be back.

Chapter 2
What is going on?

Stephen and I drove as fast as we could into the centre of Reading. It was after all, the Friday rush hour and everybody seemed to have the same idea, getting in our way. I knew the multi-storey carpark was expensive and I knew, if we were to be long, that we would soon run out of money in a pay and display. I knew of a local street where we could park for free and we rushed from there to A+E, where we met the ambulance driver just coming out. He ushered us into a waiting room and eventually the senior A+E doctor came and asked me what had happened.

I had to refer to Timothy and Stephen, as they knew more than I did, and they told him what had happened and how they had dealt with the situation. They had arrived home to find their mother's car still on the drive and the front door not locked. They called for their mother, but when there was no reply they wondered if she had gone for a walk in the snow. However, their logic told them that she would have locked the front door and so they went to look around the home for her. They found her on the bedroom floor where she had probably laid since about 8.00am that morning and they came home at 3.25pm. Timothy immediately made the emergency call and kept his mother alive with the finger squeeze and other instructions and reassurance he received on the telephone from the emergency services until the paramedic arrived.

We were then allowed in to see Helen. She was in even more distress than before and was not even recognising us, though there had been some recognition at home. The medical team explained that they had arranged to transfer her to the John Radcliffe (JR) hospital in Oxford where a Neuro surgical team were waiting for her. The doctor explained that they had done a CT scan and she had a major bleed in her brain and she was also suffering from Hydrocephalus (excessive fluid build-up on the brain) which was compressing her brain and so causing the distress. The doctor then explained that they were going to intubate (put to sleep on a life support system) Helen for the transfer and that this would occur under blue lights and that it was unlikely that we would be able to see her once she had arrived at the John Radcliffe. We were again put into a waiting room whilst they put Helen to sleep and then we were allowed in again to see her before the transfer. Why did it take so long to put her to sleep?

We were then told to make our way to the John Radcliffe. Where is the JR? Not knowing the way, a helpful nurse printed off some Google map instructions which involved the A34, but I knew this was blocked due to a lorry having overturned. The only other helpful (!) instruction was turn right at Sainsbury's and then follow the signs to A+E. We didn't find Sainsbury's for at least a couple of days.

We went back to the car and set off for Oxford expecting the ambulance on blue lights to be ahead of us. Once we hit the countryside on the A4074 to Oxford the outside air temperature was hitting about -2°C and the snow was now settling on the side of the road and filling the central reservation in some places. A blue lighted ambulance caught us up on the outskirts of Oxford and we just knew Helen was onboard.

When you arrive at a new hospital where do you go? We followed the inner prompting to park in the carpark for the West Wing at the JR. We went in and up to the second floor where we reported to the Neuro Science Ward and a very nice nurse took us down to Neuro Intensive Care (NICU) where she introduced us to the reception team. We were taken to the relatives' room to await bring spoken to. Just before 10.00pm the surgeon (who I was later to discover was the top man in his field in the south of England) and his Senior Registrar came to see me, without the children, and he said there was no choice but to operate on the bleed in Helen's head. If they did not operate, she would die in the next couple of hours. He also said he hoped that he would not need to see me before the surgery had finished. I will openly admit I did not fully understand the significance of this statement, but I later did!

I learned that the surgeon normally goes home on a Friday evening, but on this occasion, he had not gone home! What a difference it would have made if he had needed to be called back to the hospital. There was no other operation currently under way, and there was a spare bed in the Neuro Intensive Care Unit. Had they needed to make a decision between Helen, who had been collapsed on the floor for about eight hours, and someone with a recent injury who would they have chosen? The empty theatre and bed were all a mark of God's provision.

Helen had already defeated the statistics because 95% of those who have a bleed the magnitude of the one inside Helen's head, die and do not make it to A+E, we were later to be told that of those who make it to surgery, 95% do not survive the next 24 hours. Later we were shown the scans where about a fifth of her head was filled with blood and blood clot.

What I did not realise was the amount of prayer going on both at our Church and worldwide for Helen at this time. People opened their homes to groups of people to pray and they prayed into the early hours. In one home the prayer continued throughout the night.

Even more extraordinary is the fact that many of the churches in India we support were having a weekend of prayer with an early morning prayer meeting. India is 5 hours ahead of us and they started at 3.00am, just at the time the surgeons were starting to operate on Helen's head.

We then realised that we had not eaten anything since lunch apart from a chocolate biscuit. Have you tried to find food in a hospital at 10.30pm? We eventually found a vending machine which contained frozen Cornish style pasties which we had to microwave in order to eat. That was an art in itself. You wave the barcode at the microwave to set it and then quickly put in the food to cook before the microwave cooker resets! Only Timothy mastered the process. So we sat in a darkened cafeteria to eat very much alone in this vast space. Timothy and Stephen had so many questions to which I did not have an answer. Stephen later confessed that this was the first time his dad did not have any answers to his questions. I tried to maintain a sense of adventure which we were all on together, as it helped see us through what could have been a scary and frightening time for us all.

Timothy, Stephen and I were shown to the family room and were soon asleep, I was woken at 1.30am with a vision similar to Moses on the mountain when Aaron and Hur were holding up his arms so that when his arms were raised, he was victorious. I sensed the person in the vision was Helen, but I do not know who was holding her arms except that the battle was being won. I do not know how long the dream was for, but at some point, I saw her put down her arms and walk down the hill.

Almost immediately I received a call from two of the men in the Church to say they were on their way to Oxford to be with me. They arrived at about 2.15am with food and drinks. I do not drink coffee so they drank that, and they stayed about an hour to be with me and to pray with me for Helen and the whole situation. They showed me real support in the Lord.

Around 2.30am one of the surgeons appeared and asked if I would like to speak to him alone. I was not worried about privacy as the two men from the Church would find out about any outcome anyway as soon as the doctor had left me. He said that the blood clot in Helen's brain was far bigger than they had expected, but that the whole procedure had gone extremely well considering the complexity of the bleed. The bleed had occurred close to the brain stem and so there was a chance Helen would be left with a functioning brain, but no connection with the outside world or certainly limited motor function. They did not know what the outcome would be long term, however there were some nerves in the area they were working in, and that Helen might have some long term balance issues. For instance, she might never ride a bike again. He re-emphasised that the whole operation had gone extremely well. I was able to tell him that a large number of people had been praying for the whole team during the operation.

The two guys from the church stayed until just around 3.00am. About 3.15am a nurse came in to say that Helen was now settled on the ward and I could go and be with her. I spent an hour with her and then I went to get some rest for a couple of hours knowing I would need to drive home.

I dropped off remarkably quickly, and woke around 6.00am. I took Timothy and Stephen, one at a time, to see their mother and to explain to them what was going on, and to get them used to the equipment in ICU as they were going to see a lot of ICU over the next few weeks. The nurses were brilliant and a great support to myself and Timothy and Stephen and they were surprised that I took them into ICU so quickly. When I explained who had found Helen they then fully understood, and after all we were on this journey together as a family. I also discovered later on, when reading the literature for ICU, that children under 16 are not supposed to go into the ICU. Well, ours did, and I am still proud with the way they coped with the situation.

The journey home was interesting with regard to temperature. We left around 7.00am and the temperature in the underground car park was -6°C. On the journey, we recorded several places where the temperature was -11°C. We were home just before 8.00am and all went to bed. God had kept us safe despite me having been up for about 20 hours and having to drive on frozen roads for the journey back from Oxford.

I sent out an email update, as God had spoken to my heart for me to do this, and we would become amazed over the coming weeks as to where these emails ended up and who replied even once just to tell us they were praying for Helen and for us. The world is so small these days with electronic mail.

Just before I went to sleep God reminded me of the verse from Genesis 50:20 *"You intended to harm me, but God intended it for good to accomplish what is now being done, the saving of many lives."* What God was going to do, we did not know, but I knew one thing. God was in control. Did I blame Him? No, I just knew this was to be a journey and I knew He was in it.

Chapter 3
Now go and establish your own routine.

There are those who are angels in disguise who will offer their help uncompromisingly to fellow believers. I received a call from one of those about midday on the Saturday offering to take us back to the JR in the afternoon. Even when their car had packed up, they borrowed a neighbour's car to take us. Little did I realise how tired I was, as I slept both ways.

We were introduced to the nurse who would be with Helen for the next 3 days. She was brilliant and explained in detail the care being offered along with the drugs being used and their purpose. Timothy was fascinated by the drugs and dosage (after all he does want to be a medic) and Stephen was taking in all the technology being used (he does want to be an engineer). Both of them soon learned to read the machines and what the figures meant in regard to Helen's progress.

This nurse offered me the following advice, "When you go home, establish your own routines for all the domestic duties very quickly". She told us not to be tempted to tidy up the house because when Helen wakes up and we cannot find anything she will remember where it is. How true that was to prove later.

They had decided not to attempt to wake Helen up but to give her brain at least another 24 hours rest. They did, however, reduce the level of sedation to a point where she was starting to move her legs and arms. This was such a good sign that things were starting to work again and messages were going from her brain to her limbs. They removed a cannula from one of Helen's hands and she reacted quite strongly to the pain.

What was more interesting was her reactions to me, Remember, of course, that she was still quite heavily sedated. When I spoke to her she raised her eyebrows slightly, so I asked her, that if she knew who I was, would she do that again. I also told her that if the answer was yes to a question to raise her eyebrows, which she did again. I asked her to frown if the answer was no. We then proceeded to have some form of communication like this. This amazed the nurse as Helen was supposed to be sedated. The bible tells us about the three-fold nature of man, spirit, soul and body. It also talks about a man and woman, once married being one flesh (soul). Helen knew I was there with her and she was able to respond to me talking to her and I was able to assure her of our love for her. She also responded to Timothy and Stephen. The sedation was working on her body, but her soul was able to respond to those who had the appropriate relationship to her.

We were able to pray with Helen at this time and the nurse had obviously not seen this before, so I was able to tell her of our beliefs and that very many people were praying for Helen and the people looking after her. The nurse was amazed at the sense of peace around the bed and that so many people might be concerned for one person who was so ill. I was able to share a bit about our belief in the power of prayer and that God still heals today.

Again the 'angel' took us home. It is hard to believe that just 24 hours ago our life took such a dramatic turn. Once home, we ate and went to bed. Sleep did not come easily to any of us.

Chapter 4
Sunday what can we do but praise you?
(Sunday 12th February 2012)

We went to Church on Sunday morning. We had been invited out for lunch and we all wanted to be with the Church family. The praise and worship was just what we all needed. Our praise and worship leader was spot on that day. "One knows when there is a witness of the Holy Spirit as the people of God praise him not with froth and bubbles but in sincerity and openness of heart." The words of many of the songs really moved me and lifted me up at the same time. Many people, just came up to me and said they had been praying and Timothy and Stephen were so glad to be amongst their friends from the youth group. It was amazing how many people had been in prayer for many hours for all of us.

After lunch, we set off for the John Radcliffe. The snow was starting to melt and the crops in the fields were again starting to show through the snow. The British countryside is beautiful when covered in snow. In fact, it is beautiful in all seasons. I had been in touch with the JR Neuro ICU in the morning and Helen had been comfortable all night and her limb movements had increased. They had decided to remove all the sedation in the morning and so, when we arrived, Helen was certainly looking better with a bit of colour in her cheeks. We had learned to read the screens by now and we could see that Helen was driving the ventilator rather than the other way round and it was providing the minimum level of support, but sufficient to keep her cranial pressures correct and her oxygen saturation at the right level. Helen continued to respond to our presence although she was not opening her eyes voluntarily. Physically she seemed to be still asleep, but we knew she was in there. Helen started to cough just before we left and she responded strongly to their attempts to remove the gunk. We understand this is a good sign, but the distress she suffered was something we were going have to get used to. They did not plan to put Helen back on the sedation and they did not want to remove the breathing tube during the night which meant if she started disliking the tube they would have to restore the sedation to get her through the night. She had also started to move her legs and we later discovered that she hated those lovely white stockings they fit to prevent blood clots in the legs. This was a fantastic sign that her brain was connecting to the rest of her body. Whilst the movements were not coordinated, it was a clear indication of brain to spine connectivity. Helen had started to squeeze my hand when I put mine to hers, but we later learned that this is a reflex action and does not necessarily mean that the response is a voluntary one.

The drive home seemed so long, and in the dark, we had yet to establish all the appropriate landmarks into place which would make this journey seem to pass more quickly. When we got home, the house was in darkness and the heating had not kicked in. There were many messages on the answer phone and there were several to follow up. We received offers of food from people within the Church for different days, all of whom needed replies. It took several hours to sort all this out and to get the domestic sorted. We all collapsed into bed and I certainly dropped off quickly, but was awake several times during the night.

We were all so appreciative of the love shown to us at Church and from across the world and to know that so many around the world are praying for Helen.

God gave me the verse from Genesis 50:20 - *"You intended to harm me, but God intended it for good to accomplish what is now being done, the saving of many lives."* - We do not know what else will be accomplished as a result of so many people being united in prayer

Chapter 5
Reality dawned.
(Monday 13th February 2012)

I woke early and realised that half of the bed was empty. Helen was not there and I suddenly remembered the events of the last two days. I knew I could not reasonably ring the JR before 8.00am, but I was desperate for news. I duly rang and received very little more news that I did not already know from yesterday. The washing machine had finished its first load and was loaded again. Oh, the joy of domestic tasks, but reality was starting to really sink in. That was the school uniform washed for half term, only my shirts to do and then we would be ready. The nurse was right, get your own routine running. We had an early lunch and then headed for the JR. The journey seemed so different now that the snow, which had been to the road edges had started to thaw and the roads were damp with mud kicking up continually filling the rear window. It was a good job I had topped up the washer bottles on both cars only the weekend before.

On arrival, the ward administrator told me that we could have free parking, but I would have to collect the pass from the nice lady in the security portacabin. What an interesting walk down four floors, walk 100 metres, up five floors and then a long walk through the hospital. Then the journey in reverse. The ward administrator also gave me a 'sick note' for Helen, signing her off for twelve weeks! Was Helen really going to be ill for this long? If I am honest panic set in at that point. How would we survive?

Then I realised the wonders of man's creative inventiveness. I was amazed at all the technology that was keeping Helen alive: a respirator to help her with breathing, drug dispensers, some of which were computer controlled, depending upon how she was responding and all that monitoring equipment which responded so quickly to any readings outside the set parameters.

Helen had been comfortable over night, but had become 'too tube tolerant' and so they took her to theatre again at lunch time to fit a tracheotomy tube. This enabled the staff to drain her lungs more easily and to 'degunk' her as appropriate. She found this process uncomfortable and was moving her arms around more freely. She was also moving her legs around the bed. She started to respond to my voice and when I rubbed her legs she obviously found this comforting. They had put her on a general antibiotic to try and clear her chest. We were led to believe that she had probably inhaled some of her vomit whilst she was on the floor. This is not unusual, but until they know what the infection is, this will be the procedure. They were also reducing the level of oxygen to just above atmospheric levels and the ventilator would be used for breathing support until all the drugs wore off and she came fully round. By 5.00pm Helen was completely off any anaesthetic drugs and they recommenced feeding (via a tube down her nose). She was still not breathing for herself. Timothy and Stephen were getting used to the technology surrounding their mother, Timothy was particularly interested in the drugs and their uses and also the statistics and what they were showing about Helen's medical condition. After all, as I mentioned before, he did want to become a doctor. Stephen was interested in how the various pieces of technology worked and how they all linked together.

The nurse who was looking after Helen during the next three days was on a break from Afghanistan and was an ICU nurse who had been involved in moving very sick soldiers back to Camp Bastion before accompanying them back to the UK. She gave us some true insight into the real situation out there and she was the most helpful at informing us about Helen's progress and treatment. She was very positive about the possible prognosis, and we were able to share with her a little about ourselves.

When we returned home, I received an email quoting Ephesians 3:20 *"Now unto Him who is able to do exceedingly abundantly above all that we ask or think, according to the power that worketh in us."* The person who sent me this email was to send several more over the months which were a real encouragement and always 'spot on'.

At 9.30pm I received a call from the JR to say that they had taken Helen for another scan as the drain from her brain did not appear to be working and they might need to relocate it, which would require another operation. They rang back at 10.15 to say that there was no fluid build up, but they needed to fit a pressure sensor so that they could monitor the pressure within Helen's brain, which they had been previously doing via the drain. So Helen went back to theatre again for another operation and more anaesthetic.

Chapter 6
Routine must reign.
(Tuesday 14th February 2012)

Ephesians 3:20 *"Now unto him that is able to do exceeding abundantly above all that we ask or think, according to the power that worketh in us."*

As I was reading Proverbs 4, verses 20 - 22 struck out *"My son, attend to my words; incline thine ear unto my sayings. Let them not depart from thine eyes; keep them in the midst of thine heart. For they are life unto those that find them, and health to all their flesh."*

- may we see this evident in Helen's life.

Psalm 37:1-6 is a wonderful read. *"Do not fret because of those who are evil or be envious of those who do wrong for like the grass they will soon wither, like green plants they will soon die away. Trust in the* LORD *and do good; dwell in the land and enjoy safe pasture[4] Take delight in the* LORD, *and he will give you the desires of your heart. Commit your way to the* LORD; *trust in him and he will do this. He will make your righteous reward shine like the dawn, your vindication like the noonday sun."*

On a practical level we were now getting into a routine and we were so glad it was half term so that we could get our lives sorted. The call to the JR in the morning said that Helen was much more responsive and that they were going to start the process of weaning her off the ventilator during the morning.

The morning was spent doing various domestic tasks before we set off for the JR. I hoped we would not get too used to this journey from Reading to Oxford. Already the boys were starting to name markers along the route to indicate where we had got to, the pig farm - with no pigs just a big sign saying 'Eat pork', the tractor shop - which Stephen wanted to visit, and RAF Benson trying to see if the air ambulance was on the ground. For me, it was the large, illuminated sign to indicate the start of the dual carriageway at the start of the Oxford ring road.

When we arrived, the staff had moved Helen to Bay one which had a lovely view from the window and, more importantly for Stephen, a view of the heliport. Helen was much more mobile now and she opened her eyes when we spoke to her, but quickly closed them again. We came to realise that every time she opened her eyes she did not know where she was or how she got there. This must have been a frightening experience, but by the grace of God, she did not remember any of this time in intensive care in later days. She was now triggering the ventilator herself and the machine was just providing support. Stephen told her that we had come in her car and that "Daddy had made it all mucky." Helen pulled a face at this point, much to the surprise of the nurse with her. The old Helen was still in there somewhere, we just had to get to her. Certainly, she responded to Stephen's comment about her car. She had bought it new in November and up to this point had only managed to put less than 1000 miles on the clock. That was to change with a round trip to the JR being around 100 miles and so I decided to share the mileage between our two cars.

Helen's oxygen saturation levels had improved faster than they had expected. There was still gunk on her chest, but this appeared to be clearing and she was responding more overtly to having the suction tube put into her lungs. She had been for another CT just to check on the fluid levels within her skull and to check that the drain was working. This was not the Valentine's Day we had planned for this half term. I took Helen her card which she duly held for about a minute and then dropped it when she closed her eyes. The nurse picked it up and put it on her unit.

We returned home this evening to a card through the door from someone who works in the village post office and I quote, "This is to really let you know lots of people you may not know very well and many you do not know are praying God's blessing on you at this very difficult time, especially for Helen's recovery." I had been to the bank in the morning and a lady behind the counter said she had prayed for me the previous night!

Wednesday 15th February 2021

When I woke about 7.00am, God spoke to me from Psalms 23 v 4 - 5 *"Even though I walk through the valley of the shadow of death, I will fear no evil for You are with me, Your rod and staff they comfort me."* God reminded me of the message I gave at the Bible Week this year about valleys. Then the post arrived with a card from some parents from school, whom I had lost touch with. They quoted from the whole of Psalms 23 posted two days ago, with the emphasis on the beginning of verse 3, *"He restores my soul"*. God is good and confirms His Word.

We were awake early and so I was able to contact the JR before the shift change. I had already learned that in order to get accurate overnight information you have to make contact before the shift hand over period, which starts about 30 minutes before the shift ended. Helen seemed to have slept for most of the night but had woken up about 5.00am. This was to become a pattern for quite a period of time. Interestingly enough, I had also been awake at 5.00am and spent the time in prayer before dropping off again.

When we arrived in the early afternoon Helen opened her eyes to see who was there and there was more recognition of who we were. When a patient is in intensive care there are no real visiting hours, but the JR operate a system of a blackout period between 12.00 and 3.00pm which they have found really benefits the patients, where all the blinds are drawn and all the lights turned off. Visitors are also asked to leave the ward unless given specific permission to remain. I was asked why I did not visit in the mornings as well during that first week. Well, I did have Timothy and Stephen to think of and what would we do with that three hour period in the middle of the day? Timothy and Stephen were very much on side at that time and I did not want them to become bored with visiting their mother. I could have spent all day there, but it would not have been right for their sakes.

I encouraged the boys to just talk to her about what was going on and how they felt. They had removed the drain from the rear of her head as it was no longer doing anything and it was clear that the fluid was draining from her brain naturally. It was explained to me that it was unusual to be able to do this so soon after such a big internal bleed! Again, this was a sign of the healing from above that was going on. The staff had assessed her as being 10 on the Glasgow Coma Scale (GCS) and she was moving her hands to various parts of her body. These were all good signs that the whole of Helen's brain was working even if some of her movements were not very coordinated at this time.

During that afternoon she was becoming more awake all the time and she was recognising voices and starting to turn towards the voice. Her chest was certainly clearer and she did not cough at all whilst we were there.

Then we had a surprise visit from a doctor friend of ours who was working in Oxford. He greeted her with "What are you doing here?" This produced wide open eyes and an expression of "I do not know". He was amazed at her progress to date considering how she had been on the previous Friday. That doctor friend was to become a real support over the coming weeks and he will never really know how much his support meant to me. His wisdom, common sense and of course his medical knowledge were invaluable on occasions.

Chapter 7
The Ventilator Must Go
(Thursday 16th February 2021)

I received the following from some good friends near Worcester overnight, Psalms 41:3 *"The Lord will strengthen him on his sickbed and restore him from his bed of illness"* - what a fabulous verse of both strength and restoration.

The end of that Psalms 41:11 - 13 *"I know that you are pleased with me, for my enemy does not triumph over me. Because of my integrity you uphold me and set me in your presence forever. Praise be to the LORD, the God of Israel, from everlasting to everlasting. Amen and Amen."*

The morning call to the JR told us that Helen seemed more awake and they were going to try and get her off the ventilator during the day. This would prove to be a major step in her recovery and her independence.

When we arrived in the afternoon they had already removed the main Intravenous line from her chest, as well as the head pressure monitor and her pressure had stabilised to the point where they no longer considered it necessary. The nurse was really surprised by the progress Helen was making. Helen was opening her eyes even more and she had started responding to questions from the nurses and ourselves. She clearly knew who we were and was responding differently to what we were saying. She was also turning toward the speaker. During the morning she had been sat upright by the Physiotherapist and she was able to support herself with minimum intervention.

Whilst I was there they decided to remove her from the ventilator and allow her to use a trachi mask. (This is done when someone is first removed from the ventilator and they have a tracheostomy, as otherwise the air they breathe in will be too dry and the oxygen level too low. A trachi mask is like a face mask, but the air mix supplied is at atmospheric pressure.) She initially found the lack of ventilator a bit distressing and was trying to bring her hand up to her face, but she quickly settled to breathing on her own, a dampened and oxygen enriched air supply. Her stats quickly settled down and her oxygen saturation was at 98% and her pulse and breathing rate settled to what it had been before removing the ventilator. Her GCS readings were up to 11 and at some point she had a release of gas from her lower bowel and I exclaimed "What was that!?" and she 'shooshed' me and smiled. Again signs that the old Helen was coming to the surface.

Her brother and his daughter had come with us and the boys had explained all about what they would see. Their eleven year old cousin found it a bit daunting initially, but Timothy and Stephen encouraged her to come into ICU twice more and Helen responded to her. This was a true mark of what God had done for the boys, in that they were prepared to explain to someone else what was going on and how their mother was progressing. Helen also responded really well to her brother and by the end of our visit she was trying to mouth things to us but we struggled to understand her.

The staff put Helen back on the ventilator at 9.30pm after 5 hours of breathing for herself. This was quite extraordinary, I was told, for less than a week from admission.

Chapter 8
To the end of the World
(Friday 17th February 2012)

Was it really only a week since this all started and half term was almost over? It seemed as if we had been on that road for a long time and yet time had flown by. There were a huge number of emails in the inbox that morning with people asking to be added to circulation list. How far are the 'Helen Update' emails reaching? One email I could see had been forwarded onto at least five people. Someone else wrote to me who I know was on a circulation list for a Church list numbering nearly 1000 people. I was truly humbled that from something which started with just telling friends had multiplied beyond all measure. People were encouraging me not to leave out the daily Bible verse. I was really only sharing what God was showing me as I walked this walk. Who knows where this would lead to and what would be the long term fruit. What kept me going was the fact that I knew people were not only praying but they were also sharing with me what God was sharing with them.

The early morning call to the JR told me that Helen was comfortable and that they were going to continue to wean her off the ventilator. This would demonstrate significant progress if it was successful.

By the time we arrived in the afternoon Helen had been off the ventilator for four hours and then they had put her back for the rest period as she was tiring. When we arrived they took her off for another four hours. This helped to clear her chest and her stats continued to improve. Her blood pressure was still high at 180/87 but her other progress was a real encouragement to the staff. She was much more facially expressive and she would move her hands to her face. She was able to stick out her tongue on command and not just a little bit! The boys told her all about the drive to Oxford and what they had been up to during the morning. They started to ask her questions about how she was feeling and she just shrugged her shoulders. Just before we left they put her back on the ventilator and then gave her another hour off it in the evening. That would total nine hours breathing on her own on the first full day of trying, a real miracle in itself I was told.

Saturday 18th February 2012

I was encouraged by Psalms 116:1- 2 *"I love the Lord, for he heard my voice; He heard my cry for mercy. Because he turned his ear to me, I will call on Him as long as I live."* This reminds us that God hears us when we call out to Him and that he wants us to commit our lives fully to Him in everything we do.

Helen was restless and wanted to get out of bed. When we arrived, she was trying to vocalise words to us. She had been off the ventilator since early morning using only the trachi mask. Timothy was fascinated by what was in the feed they were giving her, but declined to try any when offered. The brown mix looked very unappetising. The doctors were a bit concerned by Helen's restlessness, but a CT scan had not revealed anything abnormal so they were happy. Her BP was still a bit high at 182/89, but her temperature was much better. She had her eyes open about 50% of the time we were there and she mouthed words to us. She wanted hugs from us all! In the late afternoon she started to ask the question "Where am I?" This was a really good sign that she was starting to think actively and not just reactively to her situation. Leaving was difficult as she became upset that we were going, leaving her there. We spent nearly five hours in the hospital and we began to realise that we were also getting into a routine. Whilst this was good, I trusted this was not going to be forever. We did not have a good journey home as the traffic was slow for a Saturday evening.

Sunday 19th February 2012

I returned to Psalms 116 this morning vs 8 - 9 *"For You have delivered my soul from death, My eyes from tears and my feet from falling. I will walk before the Lord in the land of the living."* Certainly verse 8 is our experience and verse 9 should be for all of us forever. This reminds me to ask, are we all walking before the Lord or are we walking for ourselves? If you are walking for yourself please turn and totally commit yourselves to walking before God.

For us as a family, Sunday has always been the focus of the week with our full commitment to the Church where we have served God for nearly 30 years. It is the place where Helen and I met, married, had our children dedicated and, over the last few years, saw them baptised by immersion. The three of us went knowing that Helen was still very ill in hospital and I guess the reality of the situation hit home. All the washing was completed, the ironing done and we got up early as we had been invited out for lunch before heading off to Oxford to visit Helen. There are people in the Church who will never know how much their help in small and large ways really blessed us.

I made the usual morning call to find out how Helen had been overnight and she had been doing so well that they did not need to put her back on the ventilator during the night. She was breathing strongly and her oxygen saturation was very good, particularly her saturation levels.

When we arrived, she was in the chair, where she had been all morning, and then again after the midday rest session.

The physios had been to see her and she stood up taking her own weight and she was able to get into a standing position using her arms from a chair. All the people who are 'in the know' say this is remarkable for someone who had suffered a brain injury like Helen's. She had also been pulling herself up in bed and had attempted to roll over in the night several times, again all good indicators. Her temperature had started to go down which was a good sign that the chest infection was now coming under control, but the fact that she had now been off the ventilator for a significant period helped to clear this up as well.

They also decided to deflate the cuff on the trachi tube which meant that Helen was now in a position to start drinking small amounts of fluids. She had been asking for a cup of tea for about 24 hours and so the nurse started to give her water on a sponge on a stick. It was obvious that Helen was very thirsty and so eventually the nurse allowed Helen some water from a cup, which she did mostly herself. A bit went the wrong way, but she was able to deal with this.

It was significant that she was clearly localising to her face with her hand movements. She had always hated having her hair on her face and during the afternoon, a couple of times a hair had become stuck to her face. She was clearly locating this and then removing it herself, indicating that her fine motor skills were returning. She had been given a Glasgow Coma Scale of 14 due to her speaking. Helen did complain of having a headache which we were told would ease. Her temperature was returning to normal.

Chapter 9
Half Term is over
(Monday 20th February)

Joshua 1:5b *"As I was with Moses, so I will be with you; I will not fail you or forsake you."* and Mark 3:11 *"I say unto thee, Arise, and take up thy bed and go thy way into thine house."*

Back to school. We were all up very early to ensure that we had everything in place for the three of us to return to school. Bags had been packed the night before and we had all made our sandwiches. The extra food for our visit to Oxford was ready. I left just after 7.00am as I had a meeting with my line manager as she wanted to check that I was ok. Timothy and Stephen were going to have to see themselves out and lock up the house. How they had grown up in the last week! There were times when I was so proud of them and I knew their mother would be when she realised what they had been through. I did email their school to give them a heads up about the situation (but as I subsequently discovered the email did not reach all the appropriate parties). My meeting at school went very well and they offered for me to leave early two days a week. I did not teach last lesson on those days, so that gave me some time to sort things out. I could not believe how supportive they were, with all the support plans they were offering.

The school day flew by and I picked the boys up at the end of their day. We started our drive to Oxford. We were over an hour later than the previous week and this made significant difference to the traffic. Helen was awake and waiting for us although she still did not really have any sense of time. The speech and language therapy staff assessed her swallowing ability and did not consider her safe to swallow but would reassess the situation tomorrow. They had planned to move her onto the ward, but her temperature was up a bit and so the move would have to wait. They put her onto a different antibiotic for seven days to finally clear any infections.

When we arrived, she had been in the chair for three hours. She started asking questions today which was a significant indicator of how her brain was doing. "Have I been here long? Have I been very ill?" she asked. When we answered she became a bit upset and started saying sorry for being a trouble.

Helen said that the nurse was a very nice lady and she had managed to persuade the nurse to let her have some tea in a cup. The one inch of tea disappeared in an instant and then she started asking what the time was. Again all good indicators that Helen was starting to think about things. By early evening she was starting to tire and I knew we had to get home. Fortunately, dinner was in the fridge and only needed reheating. This was the start of many dinners provided by a small group of members of the Church. We had been randomly offered meals during the previous week, but someone had taken on the rota so that all we had to do was collect the meals from a central point and then reheat either a full meal or add rice or pasta to what was provided. What a blessing this was to become and what a variety of food!

Tuesday 21st February 2021

This was a full teaching day at school for me and I made the morning call to the hospital at 7.30am. I had worked out that the key time to ring was before handover started from the night staff to the day shift. The nurses did twelve-hour shifts which meant that the patients in ICU only needed to get used to two staff every 24 hours which certainly worked well for Helen, saving confusion as there was enough to confuse her anyway. Helen had slept well and her stats had been stable overnight. She had woken at 5.00am (just the same time as me – more about that later) and had started to ask when we were coming to see her. Despite the lack of any real short term memory she was asking staff when we were due to arrive. The brain is a fascinating thing.

We duly arrived mid-afternoon to visit and it was obvious that she was much better than the previous day and much more awake. The format for the visits was for me to go in first and establish how Helen was and then for the boys to visit on a fifteen-minute rotation with them both being allowed in for the last session. There were times when there were more than three round the bed particularly when our consultant friend visited her. Helen immediately asked where Timothy and Stephen were and I explained that they would be in soon. She wanted to see them NOW so of course we obliged. Her BP had improved to 135/82 and they had replaced the internal trachi tube so that she could speak more easily. Whilst we were there, they took her off the trachi mask and tried her on a trachi valve which enabled her to speak almost normally. She consumed two yoghurts for lunch 'with vigour' and the nurse was very pleased with her progress. She still needed to be careful with fluids and they were going to reassess her on Thursday. She started to be involved with her own care and had been applying body lotion to her face and arms and she had been brushing her hair. She had her eyes open for more of the time and she was able to remember when her birthday was. The nurse had a chat with me about Helen's short-term memory which did not seem to be working very well, if at all, and time was a complete mystery to her. She kept asking what had happened to her and I began to understand what it must be like, when every time you open your eyes you do not know where you are or what has happened to you.

She had also had a visit from her sister and Helen was insistent on praying with her.

Just before we left, the staff put Helen back in the bed as she had been in the chair for five hours which was far longer than they expected for her. They got her to stand up and then transfer herself back to the bed! Her balance had improved significantly since the previous day.

Wednesday 22nd February 2021

Psalm 117 just seemed right for today. *"Praise the LORD, all you nations; extol him, all you peoples. For great is his love toward us, and the faithfulness of the LORD endures forever. Praise the LORD."*

Helen had a good night and wanted a cuppa when she woke around 5.00am and again started to ask about 'her boys'"– the ones in the photos. To explain. On the day after Helen's collapse Timothy had found a photo of myself and the boys and made it into a get-well card. Helen then started to refer to us as her boys. I must add that this card went missing several times, but we always managed to locate it.

We arrived mid-afternoon, but Helen wasn't in ICU – panic – she had been moved onto the ward! This was such amazing progress for one who had been so ill on admission. We found her tired, but in a room on her own. She had been to the gym with the physios and had walked 30m unaided which really surprised the staff. However, she was not eating and this was a cause for concern and so the staff were considering fitting a feeding tube directly into her stomach. This became a matter for prayer, but they left it for a couple of days more to see how she might do. They were also considering moving her back to Reading hospital and they would not take her with a trachi tube still in. She was quite confused today and she had not coped too well with the move to the ward.

Our consultant friend came in and he was blown away by her progress. He was his usual cheeky self and we saw Helen's humorous/rude replies to him, something of the old Helen. She told us she had fallen on the floor and that was why she was in hospital and she told me that there were some mucky clothes of Stephen's on the floor in front of the washing machine which needed to be washed. I assured her that we had now done them. She also remembered that Timothy wanted to be a doctor and Stephen an engineer.

Thursday 23rd February 2012

Psalm 118:1-5 today *"Give thanks to the LORD, for he is good; his love endures forever. Let Israel say: "His love endures forever." Let the house of Aaron say: "His love endures forever." Let those who fear the LORD say: "His love endures forever." When hard pressed, I cried to the LORD; He brought me into a spacious place."* What a set of verses and one can repeat the repeating phrase.

I also received the following from a friend "this morning whilst praying for Helen and family, the good old song came YOU PLOUGH THE FIELDS AND SCATTER came to mind and I found myself singing it a few times through the day. Yes Helen has ploughed a furrow across the field, but how many seeds have been sown, about God's marvellous powers, not only to Christians but to non- believers, worldwide we will never know!"

Helen did not have a good night and had finally settled around 2.00am. She then slept until 6.00am which was late for her. She was finding all the new faces hard. When she was in ICU she had one nurse who was responsible for her and now on the ward there were very many different faces. We were told that, all being well, they planned to remove the trachi tube tomorrow. Helen was quite chatty and she was finding swallowing easier and so they were allowing her to drink tea from a "child's style" beaker. They proposed to allow her to start on proper (soft) food so long as she could be supervised. Oh the JR is so far away for people to supervise her. She went to the gym today and just kept going on the treadmill until the physios thought she had been far enough. Again, significant progress. She was trying to remove the last tubes and so they were keen to get her eating and drinking independently. She had her eyes open for most of the visiting session.

Chapter 10
Is it really two weeks?
(Friday 24th February 2021)

Psalm 119:49-50 *"Remember Your Word to Your servant, for You have given me hope. My comfort in my suffering is this: Your promise renews my life."*
I have really hung onto these words today.

It is amazing how things, can vary. The journey to the JR was a typical Oxford Friday with cars stationary and when you thought you could move, the lights went red! I had really brought the wrong car today. Whilst Helen's car is very economical, its small engine and clutch are not very good in stop/start traffic. My diesel will just crawl along in first gear and idle for miles. Remind me not to use the ring road on a Friday again!

When we arrived, Helen was very confused about everything and kept referring to the hospital as a prison. She had been moved to another room and that did not help her. Her independent streak was starting to show itself and yet Helen was not in a position physically to be independent. The staff had taken her to theatre in the morning to remove the trachi tube and that had made a real difference to her ability to speak. It was two weeks since her collapse and we had to remember how far she had come.

The nursing staff were concerned that she was not eating or drinking enough. She was saying that the water was warm and they would not let her have a cup of tea. The good thing was that she did have room with a view, even if over the graveyard, but from the bed she could not see that. We tried to stay as long as we could but the first week back at school had made us all very tired and so we left around 7.00pm. Helen did not want us to leave as, again, she referred to the prison, but we assured her that we would be back tomorrow. She told us that was a long time away. We were so torn! Timothy and Stephen found the drinks machine. I am not sure they were supposed to help themselves. At least the journey home was easier.

Saturday 25th February 2012

Psalms 119:41-43 *"May your unfailing love come to me, LORD, your salvation, according to your promise; then I can answer anyone who taunts me, for I trust in your word. Never take your word of truth from my mouth, for I have put my hope in your precepts.*

Exodus 13:14 *And it shall be when thy son asketh thee in time to come, saying, What is this? that thou shalt say unto him, By strength of hand the LORD brought us out from Egypt, from the house of bondage."*

We are standing very much on the Word of God and for a great testimony of God's miracle working power.

Again, Helen did not sleep well and we arrived to find her upset. She was not eating well which became an increasing concern. She ate some soup and soft bread that I'd brought, but was refusing the high energy drinks and just wanted more tea. She had a visit from our church Pastor and his wife today and they stayed about an hour. At the weekends there were different staff and Helen was confused by this. When I tried to explain it to her, she seemed to remember, but an hour later she was asking the same questions again. The issue seemed to be with her short-term memory. She could remember increasing amounts from before her collapse, but she could not remember anything since the event. Certainly, after about an hour she did not remember receiving any visitors. When I reminded her, she then remembered the detail. I hoped this was not going to be an issue long term. Her memory from before her collapse seemed to be intact it was just accessing it which could be difficult. It was a bit like looking through a colander where you can only see through the holes and when you move it you can see other bits, but not necessarily the bits you were looking at. I just hoped the holes would get bigger.

Sunday 26th February 2012

God reminded me of this passage from Psalms 121:1-4 *"I lift up my eyes to the mountains — where does my help come from? My help comes from the LORD, the Maker of heaven and earth. He will not let your foot slip — he who watches over you will not slumber; indeed, he who watches over Israel will neither slumber nor sleep."*

Helen had a good night's sleep and she was more cooperative with her breakfast, but they struggled with her during the morning. I was never given more details and she could not remember. She had eaten some of her lunch, but again quantities were too small for their liking. When we arrived having had lunch with a Church family, she remembered that she was in hospital and that she did not want to come in again. We brought some of her clothes into hospital as they wanted to start on the physical rehab from the following day.

Helen was much brighter on our arrival and her sparkly eyes had returned. The real Helen was in there somewhere and her sense of humour was showing through. Timothy was really good with the bad jokes and the humorous bit. Her sister and daughter Lily (3 years old) arrived and Lily sat on the end of the bed and tickled Helen's toes. We all found this really amusing, particularly Helen who turned it into a real game with Lily, this seemed like a bit of a breakthrough in that Helen really perked up whilst we were there, and then very profoundly asked if she had been in hospital long and out of the blue stated that tomorrow would be Monday! The journey home was really good and we managed to get all the way through Reading on green lights, through, over fifteen sets of potential reds. The boys really were getting excited when we reached Junction 11 of the M4 without stopping and only four more sets to go (all green!).

Chapter 11
Another Week
(Monday 26th February 2021)

A verse which was to be so relevant for today, Psalms 107:27-31 in particular vs 29 - 30 *"He stilled the storm to a whisper, the waves of the sea were hushed. They were glad when it grew calm, and He guided them to their desired haven."*

Why are the school days so long? I must admit school were being really helpful and considerate and the meeting I was supposed to have at the end of the day was moved to during the day as all those who needed to be there were either free or were made free for part of the session.

When we arrived we found that Helen had been moved again to a multi-bedded ward with only an internal view. We were informed that she had been confused and agitated all day and had tried to get out of bed on her own several times. They were concerned because she was a bit unsteady on her feet. She had been with the physio to the gym twice and had made significant progress and her walking was much freer. She started to climb the stairs, but had really struggled to come down saying it was too far. Interestingly she kept mentioning France and had started speaking in French! The nursing staff quizzed me about whether we had a home in France or whether she had lived in France at some point. We have never been to France and the last French she did was in 1979 for CSE. She needed prompting to do things. She remembered us leaving yesterday and the fact that she was upset to see us go. She told us that my sister's boyfriend had sent her a card. Then became very upset about the fact that she could not remember things! This, I understood, was significant progress as when one realises what you cannot do, then the brain is definitely going into repair mode.

She spoke to me about "the man at the end of the bed", an angel who she could see and told me not to tell the boys as they might not understand. She described him in detail, taller than me, but not much, ie over six feet tall, and standing with his back to her and that he had his sword out. He had a sense of power about him and that people would not argue with anything he said. Helen told me that he was a soldier sent to keep her safe and that he could call on others if necessary. I asked her how she knew and had he spoken to her. He had been silent, but she just knew! On other occasions she told me that the sword was by his side. She said that she assumed he had armour on as she had not seen his front, but she assumed that he was smiling because she could sense it. She had mentioned him before, but I had dismissed what she had said. Her description was so detailed and convincing. Later on that year, in the summer we visited some friends in Weymouth and when she saw the sea she exclaimed that the sea was the same blue as the clothes the man at the end of the bed was wearing and again described him in the same detail! She had not remembered anything else from her first time in the JR.

She also told me in great detail about the Second Coming of Christ and quoted several appropriate hymns. This really upset her again. She told me that she kept hearing the horses coming in the distanc,e but that she was not ready for judgement and still had a great deal to do. This was a completely lucid conversation and it was difficult to imagine that there was anything wrong with her at this point except that she could see things we could not.

She was due to be referred to the RBH today, but on checking, there were no plans to make the referral this week but we were to ask again in a week's time. The hospital staff were still very concerned that she was not eating properly and that if this did not improve they would have to fit a tube into her stomach so that she could receive all the nutrients she needed for her full recovery. They were also concerned about her weight loss.

The one thing I struggled with was the lack of information available to the nearest relatives once a patient is moved from intensive care. When Helen was there, I knew the times to ring up and then the nurse tending to Helen at that point would come to the phone while another nurse took their place for a while. They were very forthcoming and I was able to get all the details I needed. Suddenly that information was almost impossible to come by. Certainly ringing up was a waste of time as no one seemed to answer the phone and even when you presented yourself to the nurse's desk they just said someone would come and see you and even after an hour you would still not be told anything useful. They seemed to forget that Helen did not really remember anything they told her and even later when she was able to write it down it was very difficult to understand what they had told her. I asked them to write in her book, but only the Occupational Therapist at the RBH later on did so.

On the way home we received a personal call from our GP to ask how Helen was getting on! He was on the phone for quite a while and whilst this delayed our final arrival home it demonstrated our relationship with him.

He had become our GP just after Helen and I married and this had been his first practice. We had seen his children grow up and his brother was a primary school teacher, eventually becoming the head of a rural school. So you can imagine that there had often been banter over the years about long school holidays and part time working! When we moved to Mortimer we asked him which of the local doctors he could recommend and he told us we could remain with him provided we did not want a home visit. We often communicated with him via email and so once Helen had been taken ill I kept him up to date with email information. Later on when Helen was in the RBH he visited her three times! Not bad personal service from one's GP.

Tuesday 28th February 2012

Proverbs 4 :20-22 *"My son, pay attention to what I say; turn your ear to my words. Do not let them out of your sight, keep them within your heart; for they are life to those who find them and health to one's whole body."*
We all need Gods Word to be health to our body, soul and spirit.

We agreed as a family that we would not visit Helen on a Tuesday as her sister did not work that day and Timothy and Stephen needed to have at least one normal day. Timothy would continue to help with cubs and then after that they both would continue to attend Explorer Scouts, all of which happened on a Tuesday. A couple from the Church who live along the road from us fed us every Tuesday evening for 16 weeks and another couple always provided us with a meal for Wednesday. They were in our home group and brought us the meal on the Tuesday evening.

We received one meal a day from a small but faithful group from the Church, coordinated by another family. This was just such a fantastic blessing - both not having to cook each day and also having the coordination of the meals taken out of our hands so as not to worry about each day. There were different styles and tastes, but they all were fantastic to us. I nearly bought a second microwave to aid the reheating process and looking back I would advise anyone in our position to do so. Anyone providing meals to someone in the same position as us needs to remember that the meals should be ones that can be easily reheated and not need significant cooking. I remember one day when we received a fantastic looking meat pie, only to be told when checking with the provider, that it would need between 1.5 – 2 hours cooking time. Some people provided complete cooking instructions with even little packets of grated cheese to add to the top for the last 15 minutes of cooking and others, packets of seasoning to add to taste.

Today's report came from both her sister and brother. She was really bright and seemed 'on the ball' when her sister arrived and Helen was very pleased to see her. She had remembered that her father had died a number of years ago and this made her upset, but she told her sister where dad had gone and so that was alright. She remembered where she lived and she recited all the months of the year. She drank independently today and remembered that she needed to eat, but was still not eating very much, which continued to concern the hospital. They planned to give her one more day before they intervened. When her brother arrived late afternoon he was very encouraged by Helen's bright welcome and she remembered that he had taken delivery of a new cooker just before she became ill. He was there during the mealtime and tried to persuade Helen to eat. She told him that he did not have the authority to make her eat! She told him she thought she had suffered a stroke like the other ladies on the ward. Today she started writing in a notebook, not very logically, but she had written down some things she wanted me to bring her. She told her brother that I would be visiting tomorrow and that would be fine!

Wednesday 29th February 2012

Hebrews 10:23 *"Let us hold unswervingly to the hope we profess, for he who promised is faithful."*

Angels are real! There are the ones we can see and the ones we cannot. Helen had a visit from a good friend of ours in the morning, who was an angel sent by God. A friend had prepared a whole load of homemade chicken soup and freshly baked bread, butter, ham, fresh fruit etc and proceeded to feed Helen for most of the day and did not give up. She arrived mid morning only to be told that visiting time was in the afternoons only. She duly informed them that she had a medical background and had come to help Helen eat. This was real wisdom as they let her in. She fed Helen until mid afternoon and this was the real break through that was needed. I was informed later that if Helen not eaten properly that day, she would have hindered her recovery as she was booked for theatre the next day to have a feeding tube fitted and that would significantly hindered her recovery. From then on eating was not really an issue.

When we arrived late afternoon one of the other ladies on the ward asked me if we had a caravan because Helen and this friend had chatted like 'a right pair of caravan widows'. The notable thing was that Helen had eaten for most of the late morning and into the early afternoon. Helen told us all about her sister's visit the day before and her friend's visit a few hours earlier! This was a 'significant memory' event and her conversation was quite logical. We left about

6.30pm after our consultant friend arrived and we left leaving them chatting.

We had only just arrived home when the JR rang to say that Helen was about to be transferred to the Royal Berkshire Hospital and transport had been arranged for 8.00pm. She should arrive there about 9.30pm and was going to the CDU (Clinical Decision Unit). Had I known, I would have helped her pack up her things. So we had a hasty meal and I headed out to the RBH so that there would be a familiar face on her arrival. She was very tired, so I did not stay long, but significantly it only took me twenty minutes to get home.

Chapter 12
The Royal Berkshire Hospital
(Thursday 1st March 2021)

This afternoon when I visited Helen her mother was with her. It had only taken me about 10 minutes to drive from school to get to the hospital. I had arranged with Timothy and Stephen that they would not visit today and that I would be home early evening to cook dinner. Helen was really quite confused and was also talking rubbish some of the time. She asked me about the lady in the next bed back at the JR who Helen said had had a stroke like her. Helen's friend visited again as the RBH was now round the corner from her children's school and Helen remembered her visit. Helen also started reciting hymns avidly although not always at appropriate times. She remembered being in the JR and was able to tell me things about the ward there. CDU was a very busy place with Helen's BP being taken very often and she said she had not slept all night.

Friday 2nd March 2012

I was reminded this evening of the verse we have written in our wedding rings; Philippians 1:6 *"being confident of this, that he who began a good work in you will carry it on to completion until the day of Christ Jesus."*
We trust God that he will completely heal Helen.

Helen's mother was able to visit her again and spent quite a bit of time with Helen before I arrived with the boys. She had been eating soft food and told me that the meals were better and she liked them. She was due to see the stroke/neuro assessment team on Monday so that they could decide on the best course of treatment. Her blood pressure seemed to have settled down and whilst she did not really like this ward she said she liked being in Reading where it did not take us so long to get home. We stayed until about 6.00pm and then went home. What a difference the 20 minute drive made compared to the usual hour or more on a Friday evening.

Saturday 3rd March 2021

As we approach another Sunday I was reading 1 Peter 5 today and I just want to quote from vs 10 - 11 *"And the God of all grace, who called you to his eternal glory in Christ, after you have suffered a little while, will himself restore you and make you strong, firm and steadfast. To him be the power/glory for ever and ever. Amen."*
God wants us to come through all the trials of life more steadfast in HIM not in ourselves.

Helen seemed much brighter today although CDU is a very busy place with people coming and going all the time a bit like a transit camp. Helen proceeded to tell me all about the previous day and her mother's visit in the morning as CDU does not have fixed visiting hours. She told me about her day so far and that she had been allowed to have a shower, though she did not wash her hair because she had a scar up the back of her head. She also proceeded to tell me all about the events of the ward and the fact that the lady in the bed opposite was due to go home and Helen told me all her details. This was quite a breakthrough as previously she had only been able to remember a few hours and certainly not events from the previous day. Helen had started to write things down and her writing improved considerably. She had started reading again albeit very slowly. She asked me to bring her in some fruit juice, primarily apple, which I had bought in the local village supermarket. Helen commented that this was an expensive way to buy fruit juice and multipacks from Asda were cheaper! We could see that her brain was starting to think logically and events were starting to have consequences as a sign that her higher cognitive functioning was starting to work again.

Sunday 4th March 2012

Helen did not sleep very well overnight and she said that the ward was too noisy for sleep. Interestingly I had not slept well either and this was to become an increasingly common pattern - that when Helen did not sleep well, neither did I. However, at least she could drowse during the day. As a consequence of the lack of sleep, Helen was rather confused again and quite weepy, although she did remember which day it was and what we usually did on a Sunday. Timothy and Stephen came with me, but the ward did not have a day room and so they quickly bored. At the JR their network was supplied by BT and so we were all able to have internet access when we were there which helped them pass some time and I was able to keep in touch with school and do some work there when Helen was asleep. We were not so fortunate at the RBH.

The doctors hoped to be able to move Helen to a proper ward on Monday and it was planned that she would start a programme of Physio. Helen did not want us to leave and so we saw her through her meal, giving her appropriate encouragement. The boys did try the train and the tunnel technique but that produced the appropriate cheeky reaction, that this technique had not worked with the boys so it would not work with her!

Chapter 13
Caversham Ward
(Monday 5th March 2012)

Psalms 127:2 *" In vain you rise up early and stay up late, toiling for food to eat, for he*
grants sleep to those He loves." So I took the medicine and went to bed.

Helen was transferred to Caversham Ward – the neuro rehab ward for the first time. She had a room to herself and she was now allowed to attend to all her personal needs herself when she wanted to. She was supposed to ring for help. but most of the time she managed on her own. Again we understood this to be significant for less than a month since such a serious brain injury. She had had a busy day by the time I arrived late afternoon as her mother, Tom and Edna H, very long standing family friends, and also Helen's friend had visited. She had written down everyone who had visited and some details of their visit, although as time progressed, she tended to forget some of the details. She remembered that someone in the Church needed to sort out their passport and all the details of that issue. She had received a visit from the consultant who said that the wounds were healing nicely and that they had taken her off the antibiotics. She still had a headache. They had come up with a plan for her to be assessed by physio, neuro psychology and neuro rehab to see if she was a candidate for their intensive rehab treatment lasting between one or two months before going home or possibly to the neuro rehab centre near Newbury.

Tuesday 6th March 2012

I went to London for the day for an important course. I read whilst on the train and was reminded of Hebrew 12 and the heroes of faith and then Hebrews 13:8 *"Jesus Christ the same yesterday, today and forever."* When I was looking it up again my eyes fell on James 1:12 *"Blessed is the one who perseveres under trial because, having stood the test, that person will receive the crown of life that the Lord has promised to those who love him."*

Helen was visited by her mother and sister and she did some physio to try and get her less 'wall huggy'. She also had a visit from our GP who, although he did not stay very long, told me by email how pleased we must be with Helen's progress.

I returned home from London to the news that someone had vandalised our caravan, levered open the door and stolen five of the windows! So Stephen and I spent the evening sticking plastic sheeting over the holes where the windows had been and talking to the police. Just what we needed!

Wednesday 7th March 2012

There was a fantastic sunset this evening and I was reminded of Psalms 113:1 - 3 *"Praise the LORD. Praise the LORD, you his servants; praise the name of the LORD. Let the name of the LORD be praised, both now and forevermore. From the rising of the sun to the place where it sets, the name of the LORD is to be praised. - let the whole earth declare the glory of God."*

Helen had a number of visitors including one couple from the Church, who brought in their 20 week scan photos to show her, and another friend. Helen remembered all the details of these visits and was able to reliably tell me all about her day. She started to have physio and Occupational Therapy and was waiting for a place on the full rehab list where she would have her own timetable and structured plan and goals. We went for a walk down the corridor to the nurse's station and they joked about her wanting another cup of tea. She was visited by our consultant friend, who was amazed at the progress Helen had made since his visit the previous week.

Thursday 8th March 2012

I want to start with 2 Corinthians 1:9-11 *"Indeed, we felt we had received the sentence of death. But this happened that we might not rely on ourselves but on God, who raises the dead. He has delivered us from such a deadly peril, and he will deliver us again. On him we have set our hope that he will continue to deliver us, as you help us by your prayers. Then many will give thanks on our behalf for the gracious favour granted us in answer to the prayers of many."*

Helen was much more tearful today and she had been awake early and had been wandering in the early hours. Apparently , had wanted a cup of tea and, after several attempts to put her back in bed, the night staff eventually decided to sit her at the nurses' station and give her a cuppa. Later on, a young doctor was struggling to use the computer and so Helen told him she could type quickly if he wanted to dictate what he wanted to say and she would type it up for him. These wanderings around 5.00am continued for several mornings. Helen also took it upon herself to entertain the night staff by reciting hymns and also recitations from Stanley Holloway which she learnt as a small child such as "Albert and the Lion".

She did, however, remember all her visitors in great detail and what they brought her. She had a vast number of cards and ran out of window sill on one ward and radiator top space. Her notice board had been filled at the beginning of the week. Today was the first time she stated strongly that she wanted to come home.

Chapter 14
Is it really one month
(Friday 9th March 2021)

2 Corinthians 1:18-20 *"But as surely as God is faithful, our message to you is not "Yes" and "No." For the Son of God, Jesus Christ, who was preached among you by us by me and Silas and Timothy was not "Yes" and "No," but in him it has always been "Yes." For no matter how many promises God has made, they are "Yes" in Christ. And so through him the "Amen" is spoken by us to the glory of God."*

One calendar month had passed since Helen was taken ill. She had much brighter eyes on my arrival and remembered in great detail all of her visitors. Two ladies from the Christian school had visited during the afternoon. She had a much better concept of time and could tell me what day of the week it was more easily. One of the things she explained to me was that she woke up and it was dark, she went to sleep and it was dark ,but when she woke up again was it the next day or the same day? It is interesting to think, how we take all this for granted and that we can tell one day form the next.

Helen still had a headache and she remembered that a headache nearly made her die. This made her really upset and say that she did not want to die. This was really interesting because later she did not remember any of this. That is why keeping notes myself was so important. Anyone reading this, who has a family member in hospital, please take copious notes as the patient will not remember all the details and will want to know what has happened later on.

Saturday 10th March 2012

I have been reading through Paul's second letter to the Corinthians; today Chapter 3 and verses 17 - 18 are relevant *"Now the Lord is the Spirit, and where the Spirit of the Lord is, there is freedom. And we all, who with unveiled faces contemplate the Lord's glory, are being transformed into his image with ever-increasing glory, which comes from the Lord, who is the Spirit."*

Today was a beautiful day and unusually mild for this time of year. We had been given a big tin of flapjacks and so I made a flask of tea in the hope that we might be allowed to find a quiet corner of the hospital to sit in the open. The boys and I took Helen to the WRVS garden and we were able to sit on a picnic bench in the sun. This was the first time Helen had been allowed outside and it was so nice. We felt like a family again for a while and just able to sit and forget that we were in the middle of a hospital. Helen still became weepy when she got tired and her walking became less stable, but we still went up and down the corridor to help with her recovery. She did not fancy the idea of trying the flight of stairs.

Sunday 11th March 2012

2 Corinthians 4:18 *"So we fix our eyes not on what is seen, but on what is unseen, since what is seen is temporary, but what is unseen is eternal."* and Hebrews 12:1b-2a *"let us run with perseverance the race marked out for us. Let us fix our eyes on Jesus"*

We all went to see Helen in the afternoon and took her a notebook to use as her own diary. Her notebooks had become a bit messy and so I removed the initial ones and we started a new one for her and dated the pages. She remembered the events of yesterday and was just able to remember where we had been for our walk. We decided to go there again and someone had given us a fresh Swiss roll to share. Her brother found us in the garden and we had a really nice time, however she was increasingly desperate to come home and also she became increasingly upset as her head was starting to hurt. This made her quite wobbly on the walk back to the ward.

Monday 12th March 2012

I went to see Helen later in the evening after an early dinner. She was asleep which, was unusual. She was difficult to rouse and very upset as her head really hurt at the back and she had pokey pains at the front. She said it felt tight like when I found her. This statement was interesting because she had never told me how she has felt on that Friday afternoon when she was taken ill before.

She was obviously in considerable pain and so I expressed my concern and they said they had rung for a doctor. This went on for quite a while with still no sign of anybody and so I continued to make a fuss. Eventually someone came and gave Helen some stronger pain medication and promised to keep an eye on her overnight. It was then nearly 11.00pm and so I went home.

Tuesday 13th March 2012

Hebrews 12 and my eyes fell onto verse 28 *" Since we are receiving a kingdom that cannot be shaken, let us be thankful and so worship God acceptably with reverence and awe."*

I rang the RBH in the morning and they assured me that Helen has slept well and that her head seemed to hurt her less. We all went to see Helen in the afternoon after school and she seemed less disturbed by her headache, although it had still not abated and I remained concerned.

Wednesday 14th March 2012

Hebrews 13:8 *" Jesus Christ is the same yesterday, today and forever"* and this is the hope to which we cling.

Helen had been for the CT scan and this revealed that there was fluid build-up in Helen's head and that she would have to be transferred back to the JR when a bed was available to have the appropriate treatment. This 'when a bed is available' or 'when we can arrange transport' was to become a real nightmare and a source of great stress.

In the afternoon, Helen and I had a detailed conversation about knitting, as she wanted to get back to doing this. We talked about the sizes of needles, and how they affect the knitting. She was generally less upset, however she started to become confused as she tired. She was struggling to read her bible and when we looked more carefully at the text you could see the text from the next page due to paper being so thin. This made it more difficult for her to read. Poor quality printing in general was not helping her reading. She was finding the transition from one line to the next a challenge, but a marker was helpful. As she was due to be transferred back to the JR the next day, we took all of her cards home. What a collection she had! The nurses stated that they had never seen so many for one person over such a short period of time.

Thursday 15th March 2012

Hebrews 13:15-16 *"Through Jesus, therefore, let us continually offer to God a sacrifice of praise — the fruit of lips that openly profess his name. And do not forget to do good and to share with others, for with such sacrifices God is pleased."* We are reminded to praise God for all he has done and to do it openly.

Helen was due to be transferred to the JR during the day, but when I checked during the afternoon, she was still at the RBH. I went to see her late afternoon. Hospital to hospital transport is problematic since it has been contracted out. If the drivers do not fancy the job, it seems they just do not do it, as was the case for Helen. Since there was no one to bring back they did not want to make the trip to Oxford with there being no chance of a chargeable return trip. She was walking much more confidently and had been drinking a large amount, most of which was tea (when she could get it). This seemed to be really helping her progress. Her brother and whole family came to visit as well and because she was in a side room, we were able to have all the visitors in together at the same time.

Chapter 15
Back to the JR
(Friday 16th March 2012)

Hebrews 13:21b "..and may He work in us what is pleasing to Him, through Jesus Christ to whom be glory for ever and ever. Amen," We have to give God the glory for all that he is doing in our lives.

I arranged with the boys that I would pick them up from school and then we would decide what to do, whether we needed to visit the RBH or the JR. I had not received any communication during the day and so I rang the RBH and at 2.00pm they told me that Helen was on her way back to Oxford. So we would be going to the JR. We had really thought that we had seen the back of the A4074 and its journey markers, but for a Friday we had a remarkably good journey. We found Helen in a side room and they had not decided what treatment to give her for her headaches. We were there when the doctor came round and he remembered Helen from before. It had, after all, only been 17 days since she was last there. He had to call for the registrar so that they could discuss what treatments to give her. He was pleased to see that she was so much better than before and that her walking had improved significantly. Helen also remembered the journey and was able to give us many of the details including their stop in traffic in Caversham when she was tempted to just get out and go to her mother's home. They suspected that the hydrocephalus had returned and to look at the source they would need to do a lumbar puncture (they needed to measure the pressure around her brain by putting a needle into her spinal cord, something that is known as a lumbar puncture) and get a sample of fluid.

Saturday 17th March 2012

James 1:5 " If any of you lacks wisdom, he should ask of God, who gives generously to all without finding fault."

We were back to the old Saturday routine with a 1.30pm departure to the JR. You always want to make the most of visiting time and the lack of parking meant there was queue. Once again we obtained a weekly ticket which meant that we could park in a staff carpark. We had learned early on that there is normally some kind of parking scheme for the relatives of long-term patients. In the case of the JR you have to pay for the ticket, but normally two days parking is covered by the cost of the weekly ticket.

When we arrived Helen had a lumbar drain fitted and the bag had already filled. She was less distressed, but her head was still hurting the same. The treatment they were giving did not seem to be making any difference. I learned that not only can too much pressure in the brain cause headaches but so can the pressure being too low. We were reluctant to leave Helen in this state, but they said they would review after the weekend. That was 48 hours away!

I went home and rang a doctor friend of mine who told me not to wait till Monday but to ring the hospital and tell them that I would be in at 10.30am on the Sunday morning and that I wanted to see whoever was responsible for her care to discuss what they were doing and what they proposed to do to make Helen better. I was to go alone and not take the boys. Also I was to be prepared to make a fuss because Helen was not capable of doing it herself.

I duly rang the hospital and told them what I was going to do.

Chapter 16
Was that an angel?
(Sunday 18ᵗʰ March 2012)

James 1:12 "Blessed is the one who perseveres under trial because, having stood the test, that person will receive the crown of life that the Lord has promised to those who love him." - This was part of today's readings and I really feel we have been under a trial, with Helen back in Oxford.

I did not sleep well that night but I arranged to drop off the boys about 8.30 am with someone from the Church and then I went to Oxford. When I arrived the place was deserted and I had trouble gaining access to the ward, so I prayed "Lord help me get in." Just at that moment, a nice person came down in the lift in full nurses uniform, got out and let me into the ward and then when I turned to say thank you she had disappeared! The staircase at that end of the JR has glass infills for the banisters, so you can see all the way to the ground floor. How did she disappear? Outside Helen's room was the junior doctor I had seen the day before, along with a couple of other senior staff, including one of the staff I recognised from the night of Helen's brain surgery. They ushered me into her room and continued chatting. My call had obviously provoked some action. The two senior staff were very casually dressed and one was in track suit bottoms and trainers.

They all came in and I asked the questions I had been given. Primarily, why could they not stop the current course of treatment and review it if there had been no change for the better after 24 hour?. Were they sure that they were draining fluid from the right place and were all the places of fluid build up connected so they could all drain?

They informed me that there was no sign of infection on the fluid they were draining from Helen and so they suspected that she had aseptic meningitis, that is an inflammation from a non-infectious cause. They thought that Helen's increased movement was causing the muscles at the back of her neck/skull to rub on the Meningeal-sack as there was a piece of bone missing at the back of her skull. Also the slow dissolving stitches had now dissolved and made some small holes through which 'brain fluid' (their term) was escaping and irritating the muscles as well. They planned to do another scan, stop the drain immediately and give Helen some strong steroids to deal with the inflammation.

They took Helen for the scan very quickly and it apparently confirmed their suspicions. They gave her some lunch along with a strong steroid and she very quickly settled down and fell asleep. I, too, ate my lunch and settled down to watch the Grand Prix on my netbook. According to the nurse I did not see much of the race. I was just resting my eyes when the nurse looked in!

Helen's head became much easier during the afternoon and a second scan revealed that the swelling was going down. We had a result! They planned to keep the drain clamped whilst they kept Helen on the steroids for a couple of days.

Monday 19th March 2012

Psalms 91:1-2 *"Whoever dwells in the shelter of the Most High will rest in the shadow of the Almighty. I will say of the LORD, "He is my refuge and my fortress, my God, in whom I trust." "*

When we arrived at the JR, Helen was very confused as to why she was there and which day it was. The nurse said that she was not really in any pain, but Helen was not convinced. They had removed the drain from her back and there was no further plan of action apart from seeing the effect the steroids would have. Helen still complained of having a headache, was rather weepy and said that it hurt to turn her head owing to the muscle irritation in the top of her neck. The nurses told her that she was not to use the toilet on her own. She had an en-suite room, but it was taking them so long to come that she had to almost ring just after she had been so they would come in time. Whilst we were there she went with me over-seeing her and as she said at least I waited outside.
Helen was feeling much better by the time we left for home and we trusted that the crisis was over.

We were told that Helen was now ready for transfer back to the RBH and they informed us that they had requested transport for the next day.

Tuesday 20th March 2012

Psalms 91:14-15 ""Because he loves me," says the LORD, "I will rescue him; I will protect him, for he acknowledges my name. He will call on me, and I will answer him; I will be with him in trouble, I will deliver him and honour him."

I would not usually visit on a Tuesday as that was covered by Helen's brother and sister, but as she was due for transfer back, no one wanted to arrive in Oxford to find that Helen had just left for Reading. That made for a frustrating day. When by 3.00pm Helen had not been moved I rang the JR to find out what the issue was and was told that there was now no transport available for that day. So I offered to drive to Oxford to collect her. However, I was told I could transport Helen, but I could not carry her notes in case I read them! I even offered to bring a box for the notes which could be sealed, but it was to no avail. So Helen had no visitors that day and apparently she had sat on the edge of the bed dressed and packed ready to go from 8.00am that day.

Chapter 17
Back to the RBH
(Wednesday 21st March 2012)

Psalms 92 :4-5 *"For you make me glad by your deeds, LORD; I sing for joy at what your hands have done. How great are your works, LORD, how profound your thoughts!"*

Helen was transferred back to the RBH today, but she lost her place on the Rehab Ward yesterday due to the delay in transporting her back to Reading. I was slightly cross to say the least. They did not know when she was to return and so they had to give the place to someone else. It was such an annoying case of lack of hospital transport and communication between hospitals.

I followed the transport progress during the day and informed the JR that I intended to visit today if Helen was not going to be transferred and that I would be annoyed if I had a wasted journey. I guess throwing my weight around at the weekend had some effect. I was assured that she would definitely be transferred today and so I should wait in Reading for her.

I received a call from a very nice nurse from the JR, whom Helen had struck up a rapport with, and who I am convinced was a Christian. She said that Helen was heading for CDU and that the nurse had actually seen the transport drive away and then rang back about 30 minutes later to say that Helen was now heading for Sidmouth Ward and that she should be there about 7.30pm. I duly set out for the RBH about 7.15 and arrived at the ward just after Helen, who as you can imagine was so pleased to see me.

Sidmouth Ward was very different from the Neuro Ward at the JR. It is a ward for gastro and critically ill patients, and not really the place for someone who should be in neuro rehab!

Helen was much brighter and she told me every detail of her day, including how she had waited with a very nice nurse in reception at the JR for the car to bring her to Reading, and she told me all about the very nice driver, where he was from and his day so far. It was as though someone had flicked a switch in Helen's brain and the connection between short term and long-term memory had been restored.

Helen had no conscious recollection of the last six weeks and only ever remembered what we told her, apart from certain events of the day when she nearly died, but that is for her to tell and not me.

She was now really on the ball and was very bright eyed. She was back with us mentally and was far less wobbly although she was still going to have to work on this area. She did feel sick and she devoured some food that they found for her. Had I known that she had not eaten properly, all day, then I would have brought some food in for her from home. She also recited to me a list of things that she would need or that she had run out of. I helped her unpack and get settled in.

Thursday 22nd March 2012

Psalms 92:8 *"But You O Lord are exalted forever"*

It rained all day and seemed such a long day. I rang the RBH in the morning, but I was unable to obtain any real information from the staff about Helen. I guess those morning calls were over. Helen seemed to be settling in well and she seemed much happier although she did not sleep well as there was too much bleeping because almost everyone else in her area of the ward was connected to some device or other. Helen's mother had visited her and Helen seemed much more contented.

Chapter 18
Six weeks have passed
(Friday 23rd March 2012)

Psalms 95:1-3 *"Come, let us sing for joy to the LORD; let us shout aloud to the Rock of our salvation. Let us come before him with thanksgiving and extol him with music and song. For the LORD is the great God, the great King above all gods."*

We do need to continue to praise God for His miraculous working power in all of our lives, particularly in Helen's life so far. It was six weeks ago today that this particular aspect of our walk before the Lord started, and we must never cease to praise Him for what He has and is doing in our lives.

Helen went for an assessment with the Occupational Therapists and the Physios and they decided to give her a stick to aid her with her walking. They suggested that she could use a walking frame, but she retorted that she was not that old! The OT came and chatted with me and said that Helen really needed to be on the Neuro Rehab Ward and not a medical one. We went for a walk round the hospital and Helen walked better than before. She was given a sheet of mental mathematics problems to do over the weekend, although the continuous distractions of the ward were to make completing it hard.

Saturday 24th March 2012

Psalms 95:6-7 *"Come, let us bow down in worship, let us kneel before the LORD our Maker; for he is our God and we are the people of his pasture, the flock under his care."*

I went on my own to visit Helen this afternoon and we went for a long walk and explored the hospital. There are only a few places you can go within the confines of a hospital. We found a garden and pond in a rather sad state in the south block, but it was nice to get into the fresh air, albeit for a short while. Just to be independent and out of the confines of the ward was great. It was also nice to be a couple again, just able to walk and chat, not be disturbed by others and just able to 'be'. I was able to talk to one of the ward staff who assured me that Helen was on the list for the Rehab Ward, but would need to wait for a place. The ward where Helen was can be a dismal place because it seems to only contain the dying. Getting out was such a luxury.

Sunday 25th March 2012

Psalms 96:8 *"Ascribe to the Lord the glory due His name; bring an offering and come into His courts."*

I went to Church with the boys and after a quick snack we went to visit Helen. I had been given a home-made Swiss Roll that was still warm and we found seats in the WRVS garden where we devoured the cake and tea we had brought. Helen's brother also turned up and so we almost had a party in the garden. It is easy to forget that this is part of the hospital. Some other people from the Church also passed by and it was nice to see them as well. The sun soon moved from the garden and we realised that it was still March as the air was chilly. So we headed back inside and the boys went off to explore the day room where someone was watching football. This entertained the boys for a while.

Monday 26th March 2012

Psalms 96:11-12 "Let the heavens rejoice, let the earth be glad; let the sea resound, and all that is in it. Let the fields be jubilant, and everything in them; let all the trees of the forest sing for joy."
Today the hedgerows went green. They were vaguely so this morning but this afternoon they have turned. Always a sign of the return of life and God's faithfulness.

A very long day at school and I am sure all the students were playing up. I went to see Helen as soon as I could get away. The boys had requested that they could go straight home and get on with their homework, so I went to see Helen before going home to cook dinner. When she was in the JR this would have been impossible. Oh, how the boys are growing up and rising to the challenges which are presented to us. Helen continued to complain of a headache which seemed to come and go. She had been with the physios twice during the day and so her walking was better than at the weekend. They had been concentrating on her walking techniques and how to recover from a stumble without falling over because she was still wobbly. She is the only one who is dressed on the ward and most cannot deal with their personal needs and the bell is continuously ringing. Helen is supposed to be supervised when she goes to the bathroom but again the delay is so long that she has taken to just nipping in when she sees that it is free.

Tuesday 27th March 2012

Psalms 98:2 *"The Lord has made his salvation known and revealed his righteousness (works - some versions) to the nations."*

This afternoon was Stephen's 'parents' evening' and a member of staff came up to me and asked how Helen was and said they had all been shocked and it had made him think and pray! All of the staff commented on how fantastic Stephen and Timothy had been and were amazed at how they had coped. Some staff did not even realise what had been going on this half-term, but commented on how both Timothy & Stephen had seemed more mature. One commented that both had spoken of God's work in their mother's life. We can only thank God for what others have seen in their lives and heard their testimony.

I popped in for a quick visit at the end of the school day as I needed to be home to transport the boys to scouts during the evening after dinner. Our GP popped in to see Helen during the middle of the day. This was his third visit. He did not stay very long, but he was really encouraged by Helen's progress. I had kept him up-to-date via email, but he wanted to see Helen for himself. He rang me just after I got home to tell me how Helen was. She had not slept very well as all the bleeping and bells had kept her awake. As a consequence she was very tired and her walking had suffered. We did not go very far for our walk just up and down the main corridor. Helen had remembered all the detail of the day and what she had done with the Physio and OT.

Wednesday 28th March 2012

Psalms 98:4 "Shout for joy to the Lord, all the earth, burst into jubilant song with music" - As we come up to Palm Sunday when we remember the entry into Jerusalem of the Passover lambs we remember the provision of Jesus as The Passover lamb.

Helen still has a headache all the time which increases and decreases. She is now on a daily physio schedule and there is one person to be discharged from Caversham Ward next week but they cannot guarantee that Helen will get the place. They did speak to me about whether we would be interested in the possibility of having Helen home for a night at the weekend. Would we! Yes! We felt it would be so nice to have her home, just for a night. They went to discuss it with the doctor who suggested the whole weekend from Friday afternoon to Sunday afternoon. I would have to do some cleaning! We agreed that I would not come and see her on the Thursday as her mother was coming in every day and her brother would be coming to visit as well. Later on in the evening she had a visit from our consultant friend who was amazed at her progress. He spoke to me about how far Helen might improve overall and he said that we needed to be realistic.

Chapter 19
Home for the weekend
(Friday 30th March 2012)

Psalms 100:5 *"For the Lord is good and His love endures forever; His faithfulness continues through all generations."*

HOME
I arrived at the hospital at 3.30pm to collect Helen and take her home for the weekend. I had collected the boys from school so they could help me with the logistics. Trying to get my head around her drug regime was interesting along with a great long list of dos and don'ts. Although the journey home was not long, the Friday rush hour probably doubled it time-wise. When we got home, Helen just walked round and put the kettle on for a 'real cup of tea' then she sat in the lounge and just took it all in. The boys made a real fuss of her making her a cup of tea and taking it in turns to make sure she was ok. We had been told that she needed to be supervised going up and down the stairs and so Timothy took that duty upon himself. We had dinner together and Helen ate the usual Friday 'oven' fish and chips really well, perhaps a bit more slowly than before. She found just being home tiring and so she went for an early night as did we all.

Saturday 31st March 2012

Psalms 101:1 *"I will sing of your love and justice; to you O Lord will I sing praise"*

We all slept really well and having breakfast together was just so good. Several cups of tea were eagerly consumed. I was having to get my head round Helen's drug regime and so I set to and produced a chart to help me keep a record of what she had taken and when. The weather was good, so we went for a walk round the village. We are particularly fortunate that the main streets of our village are on the level and there are benches in memory of people that are in just the right places. We did not need to use them, but we met people on our walk who had heard what had happened to Helen and wanted to let her know they had been praying for her. We returned for a mid-morning cuppa. For Helen it was so nice to be able to get a drink when she wanted it and not just when the trolley came round. We used the washing machine as usual, but there was not the time pressure to get everything finished before leaving to visit Helen. She managed at one point to go upstairs and then get down again without Timothy's knowledge. Timothy really told her off for doing the stairs on her own! We all smiled about this later.

Lunch was eaten as a family and I lit the stove in the lounge and soon the home was nice and warm. Then Helen went for a sleep as she was running out of steam. Timothy and Stephen then proceeded to do their homework whilst I did some of the housework and some of the school marking I had brought home for the weekend.

I do not remember what we had for dinner that day, but it was one of the meals provided from within the fellowship. Then, after dinner Helen went to have a bath. This was the first one for such a long time and she was able to have a long soak which she so enjoyed. We then spent time together as a family before we all went to bed early having had a relaxing day, without rushing to and fro from a hospital.

Sunday 1st April 2012

Romans 15:13 *"May the God of hope fill you with all joy and peace as you trust in him, so that you may overflow with hope by the power of the Holy Spirit"*. Our hope has to be in God and His continuing provision.

We all arose early as Helen was still on hospital timings and was awake shortly after 6.00am. We had planned to all go to Church as a family. It was so good to go to worship God together for what He had done for Helen in her restoration so far. So many had prayed and the group who had fed us were very pleased to see Helen. She did find it tiring and needed to get away promptly for lunch. We had Sunday lunch together and then Helen went for a sleep before we took her back to the RBH. Helen did not want to go back, but she was not well enough to be at home on her own during the week. I wrote a report on her weekend's activities for the OT and physio and took in the drug chart to show that Helen had taken all her medication and at the correct times.

Helen was almost pleading with us not to leave her in the RBH, the ward was so not right for her. The bed next to her, and one of the opposite beds was empty, so we suspected that these people had passed away during the weekend and Helen was really glad not to have been there. She had tasted death and did not want to be in the presence of those who were dying without hope. The nursing staff were impressed with the report we brought of the weekend and what Helen had achieved.

Monday 2nd April 2012

From now on, I will not be dating the days, but will summarise our weeks and weekends. We, that is the boys and myself, had started our Easter break and so afternoon visits were possible as well as visits in the evenings.

Psalms 102:1-2 & 12 - *"Hear my prayer, LORD; let my cry for help come to you. Do not hide your face from me when I am in distress. Turn your ear to me; when I call, answer me quickly." v12 But you, LORD, sit enthroned forever; your renown endures through all generations."* There was so much in this Psalm, but the two verses I have selected here seemed relevant to today.

When I arrived to visit Helen during the afternoon, I was invited to accompany her to her physio session so that I could see what she needed to do and how we could reinforce what she was doing during her treatment at the hospital. The physio was pleased to hear how Helen was good under supervision, but she had balance issues which they were going to work on and they were working hard to get Helen onto Caversham Ward (Rehab). She said that the physios were cruel as they forced her to find her own way back to the ward she was on.

They were happy for Helen to spend the weekends at home. She had spent her OT session making soup and toast and learned how to use their kitchen.

Psalms 102:27 "But you (O Lord) remain the same and your years will never end". We need to remember that God is unending and He is always the same, even when we are not.

Helen was told on Tuesday that this time she had not made it onto Caversham Ward and she was so disappointed. They took her stick away and told her she had to cope without it. This really panicked her, but it proved to be the right decision as she then made significant progress. She had an eye test which showed that her vision had improved significantly. Helen was also concerned that she had picked up that they were thinking about discharging her until a bed became available in the Rehab Ward, with the possibility of providing community support. (When she was eventually discharged from Caversham Ward it took six weeks for any community support to kick in.) Everyone who had advised us so far stated that we should refuse to let them send Helen home as once she was home she would be off the radar and they could easily forget that she was on the list. Whilst leaving Helen on this medical ward seemed cruel, she would not have coped at home on her own and that would have meant having to have someone from the family come and look after her at home. She could cope at the weekend when we were around, but she was still struggling with her short term memory and we felt that she could easily do something silly. This stand proved to be correct as I had a meeting with the Occupational Therapist on the Friday who stated that Helen still had a few cognitive issues and that she was not good at taking the initiative. Currently her instinctive reactions were not working fully and there was some concern as to what Helen would do in an emergency.

Psalms 103:1-4 *in particular v3-4 "who forgives all your sins and heals all your diseases, who redeems your life from the pit and crowns you with love and compassion,"* and many more verses from Proverbs 8 about wisdom are applicable.

On the Wednesday Helen presented me with a birthday card which she had gone to Tesco's to buy. This was a real surprise and I was really blessed by it. I was not expecting anything this year. Just having Helen alive was sufficient and her restoration was a real miracle.

Psalms 104:1 "O Lord my God you are very great; you are clothed in majesty."
I thank you for all the prayers, good wishes and cards which arrived at this time. God is very good and can turn the hearts of men (and women).

Let me say it was quite a walk from the RBH to and from the card shop and the OT and physio were really surprised how well Helen walked. She got a bit lost in the store, but found her way to the checkouts and survived. The OT stated that there might be some ongoing issues, but she would be able to manage them with training. Helen was now on the list with two others for Caversham Ward. They did say that the documentation from the weekend was very helpful and showed that the whole family was behind her recovery.

Psalms 104:33-34 "I will sing to the LORD all my life; I will sing praise to my God as long as I live. May my meditation be pleasing to him, as I rejoice in the LORD." As we start the Easter celebrations, we remember what Jesus has done for us and how awesome was the sacrifice.

We had a great weekend with Helen at home. She went to bed early as she was still on hospital timings. Saturday morning was sunny and so we went for a walk around the village and walked down a few additional side streets as well so that could check that she still remembered it all. We also went shopping in the supermarket to reinforce what Helen had been doing during the week at the RBH. She had a sleep in the afternoon and we had a great evening together as a family. On Sunday morning we went to Church and then Helen returned to the RBH late afternoon.

Monday 9th April

Psalms 106:48 *"Praise be to the Lord, the God of Israel, from everlasting to everlasting. Let the people say 'Amen!' Praise the Lord."* We remember that God is everlasting and so is His faithfulness.

We continued to support Helen in hospital. Timothy and Stephen told Helen that they were not going to visit her in hospital during the week as they had seen her for the whole weekend. They had done so well with the daily visits to both the JR and the RBH but for children, hospitals are not the most exciting places. The fact the JR had Wi-Fi made all the difference to them.

Psalms 107:20 *"He sent forth His word and healed them; He rescued them from the grave."* We can certainly see this manifest in Helen's life and talking to the OT lady she said that Helen's recovery was remarkable.

Helen had a week of short physio and OT sessions as they had to concentrate on those on the Rehab Ward. Helen had been referred to Headway the support charity who also touched base with me about what we were doing at home on her weekends with us. There was to be a Caversham Ward admissions meeting on Thursday morning and Helen was on the list to be considered for moving to that ward. We never did find out the outcome of that meeting until later on.

Psalms 108:4 - 5 *"For great is your love, higher than the heavens; your faithfulness reaches to the skies. Be exalted, O God, above the heavens; let your glory be over all the earth."*

Helen now had her mobile phone. Everyone else on the ward who could, had their mobile phone and the younger patients seemed to be continuously using their phones. We had a chat that evening and she did not do any physio as the physio came late and only chatted with her. The doctor also came to see her and said something about changing wards or being on the list to change wards, but she could not remember the detail and he did not write it in her book as the OT and physio do. We trusted it was the former after this morning's meeting. Helen did request that she be able to sleep, as someone in her bay of six had a very bad cough and was keeping everyone awake all night and she did not want to catch it. Helen was only able to walk to the doors of the ward and back today, so did not go far enough to "assess her wobbliness" – (that's in her words!)

Psalms 109:30 "With my mouth I will greatly extol the Lord; in the great throng I will praise Him." We are reminded in this Psalm right at the end that in all things we have to praise God for what He has done and what He will yet do.

Again Helen was allowed home for the weekend, we concentrated on doing the things she would need to do when she eventually came home.

Chapter 20
Teddy goes on an adventure!
(Monday 16th April 2012)

Psalms 111:2 *"Great are the works of the Lord; they are pondered by all who delight in them."*

I received a call from a very distressed Helen. We had allowed her to take her mobile phone into hospital as we were now persuaded that she would not put it down somewhere and forget where she had left it. Helen had lost her teddy. She had gone for a wash and to get dressed and when she returned the hospital staff had re-made her bed and her teddy was missing. She searched everywhere and realised that when they changed her sheets they must have scooped up her teddy as well. She asked to look through the laundry cage as she knew where her sheets were, but they refused. She was really distressed. I rang up on her behalf, but they told me that the cage had been taken away. I also rang other departments responsible for the laundry but to no avail. I managed to eventually get through to the laundry services in Dunstable and spoke to a lovely manager who initially came up with many excuses but I managed to persuade her that the teddy was important to her. She promised to get her team to look out for the teddy and send it back to the RBH.

Wednesday 18ᵗʰ April 2021

Psalms 112:1 & 8 v 1 *"Blessed is the man who fears the Lord who finds great delight in His commands"* and *v 8 "His heart is secure, he will have no fear, in the end he will look in triumph on his foes"*.

I visited Helen this afternoon and she was quite bright, her crochet blanket is growing quickly. They suspect her swollen ankles are due to one of the Blood Pressure tablets she is on and so they have stopped it. (I had looked it up and had been concerned by the list of side effects.) We went for a long walk down all the corridors we could in the RBH as it was raining. We may have to start going outside to increase the distance she covers for reasons given later. Her walking was much better and more confident although she had her wobbly moments. We had a nice cuppa and discussed many things, but she can still find ordering events a challenge, although she is OK if she has written them down for herself.

The lady from the laundry, in Dunstable, rang me on the Thursday to say that not one but three teddies were on their way back to the RBH! And carefully packaged too. Some friends who live in Luton offered to go to the laundry there and rescue Helen's teddy personally.

On Monday Helen was told that she was not going to receive anymore OT or Physio on the current ward because they needed to concentrate on others. She was not sleeping well due to a change in her blood pressure medication. We replaced teddy during the week with a soft toy dog. The only good news was that they hoped that two places would come up on the Rehab Ward by the weekend.

Chapter 21
Back to Caversham Ward
(Thursday 19th April 2012)

Psalms 113:2 -3 *"Blessed be the name of the LORD from this time forth and for evermore. From the rising of the sun unto the going down of the same the LORD's name is to be praised."*

I went into the RBH today to visit Helen and went as usual to Sidmouth Ward but Helen was not there! I was told she had been transferred to Caversham Ward. This was great news. She had been there before, but this time she had been put on the formal rehab programme. I spent this visit settling her in and showing her where everything was. What a different atmosphere from a medical ward. With no bleeping of machines or buzzers going off, the staff were available to help and had time to help Helen to settle in.

Friday 20th April 2012

Psalms 113:4 *"The Lord is exalted over all the nations, His glory above the heavens."*

When I reached the RBH about 3.00pm in the afternoon Helen had been through a busy day of assessments. She had seen the Doctors, Physiotherapists, Occupational Therapists and met all the people who were going to treat her.

I went for a trip into the bowels of the RBH to recover a teddy. As I went past the kitchens where food trays were being processed, there were trays on conveyors going round and round. It was like the land of 'Umpa Loompas' from Charlie and the Chocolate Factory. Eventually, after many twists and turns, I came to the post room. There were the two teddies which had come from the laundry in Dunstable, one clearly was Helen's – the other had come from somewhere else in the RBH. When we got home I then called the lady from the laundry at Dunstable to thank her for sending back Helen's teddy. She was nearly in tears as she said nobody had said thank you to her for anything in years, they only ever rang up to complain. I also shared with her that people had been praying for both her and the recovery of Helen's teddy. We have to trust that my brief conversation with her will have sown some seeds in her life which will come to fruit at some point in her life. Helen was overjoyed to get her teddy restored even if he did look a bit worse for wear.

Most of the staff on the Ward remembered Helen from before she went back to the JR. They said how much better she was now. She did not remember being there before or any of the facilities. We went through the formalities of her going home for the weekend, which as it was a new ward, this process took a lot longer than before.

She was not given specific homework for the weekend but there were several things we had not completed from previous weekends.

We had a great weekend at home and the routines rapidly became established. We went for a walk on Saturday, and Helen was given a greater opportunity to lead where we went. She still tired quickly, but was involved in more of the home tasks. When Helen becomes tired her balance suffers and she becomes wobbly. She really enjoyed Church on Sunday morning and she ironed some clothes before we returned to the RBH.

Her programme for the week had been left on her bed, a mix of OT and physio. We also met some relatives of the people she would be doing rehab with.

So what is rehab all about? Well I have reflected on this over a period of time, but it is all about getting you out of the system. We have discovered that the system is full of holes and once you drop through one you may never get back onto the path again. Rehab works with the patient, but there also needs to be some work done with the family. We have been so blessed with those around us who have given us input concerning what we needed to do to help Helen. There are so many assumptions made that you will know or will ask. One thing we have learned along the path is that often you do not know what questions to ask, let alone what the answer should be and whether you are being fobbed off.

Monday 24th April 2012

Psalms 115:9-11 *"All you Israelites, trust in the LORD — He is their help and shield. House of Aaron, trust in the LORD — He is their help and shield. You, who fear Him, trust in the LORD — He is your help and shield."*

Helen's first week on Rehab was mostly about assessments and getting her started. The staff were working hard on her balance and trying to ascertain what was the root cause of her balance issues. It would be something she would have to learn to manage. The Physios started a programme to work on her upper body strength as this is key to balance and to managing her posture. The latter can seriously affect balance where there is some kind of injury to the balance system in the ears. We have never really got to the bottom of whether Helen's ongoing balance issue is due to damage to the nerves during the surgery on that Friday night or whether it is a processing issue within the brain itself.

Wednesday 26th April 2012

Psalms 115:1 *"Not to us, O Lord, not to us, but to Your name be glory, because of your love and faithfulness."*

Balance is all about input from three main systems. The balance canals in the ears, input from the eyes and some inputs from the pressure sensors in both the feet and bottom depending as to whether you are standing or sitting. It also depends upon the brain processing these inputs and how quickly it can do this. Certainly with Helen her balance is not as good when she is tired, and this we discovered was to continue.

The OTs started to work on Helen's concentration and memory. It is amazing how the memory just switched back on at about the six week point. Helen was now able to remember several days at a time and certainly everything from before the bleed is available again, though sometimes accessing those memories can be a struggle and an effort.

Helen also went to see the Psychologist to try and ascertain what her cognitive processing was like. I wonder how any of us would fair with these tests? We would get the analysis within the next week.

Thursday was not a good day as they changed some of her drugs and also moved her bed. When will they understand that for some acquired brain injury patients making too many changes at once can be upsetting for the patients as well as very tiring.

Friday ended up being a bit of a high as Helen was invited to join the breakfast club, where a small group of patients plus an OT planned, prepared and cooked a breakfast for themselves. As Helen put it 'double food' at the start of the day. This turned out to be a real highlight once a week and I am not sure who learned most, the patients or the OT. Certainly, Helen's culinary skills came to the fore and they managed to fill large parts of the hospital with cooking smells. As well as her daily OT and physio, Helen also managed to get herself onto the gardening club group which looked after the ward garden and also had a vegetable patch in the physio/rehab area.

The weekend started on Friday afternoon as usual, but when I went to collect Helen she was still finishing off her activities, and so we did not get away as promptly as usual. Why did we always have to wait so long to get her drugs? For patients who are regularly going home it would be so much easier to have a weekend pack which allows the responsible carer to have the drugs in a pack ready to go or at home where medication remains the same.

Psalms 116:1-2 *"I love the Lord, for he heard my voice; he heard my cry for mercy. Because he turned his ear to me, I will call on him as long as I live."* v5 *"The Lord is gracious and righteous; our God is full of compassion."*

We have certainly experienced the compassion of the Lord and His restoration.

Again, the weekend was really productive and we continued to try and get Helen lost around the village. She was getting too good at that game and was becoming more traffic aware. Her traffic awareness had never really gone away, but we just had to make sure she would be safe when she came home and went out on her own. She just could not turn round very quickly so she has to move away from a corner to cross the road, so as to be able to see approaching vehicles from a distance and not rely on working out where cars were coming from by listening alone. We were grateful that she was able to make those decisions for herself.

Chapter 22
Another month starts
(Monday 30th April 2012)

Psalms 118:29 *"Give thanks to the Lord, for He is good; His love endures forever."*

Monday was to be a very busy day with a number of physio sessions and an OT session put in.

Helen went to a goal setting meeting where she set goals for the next couple of weeks. It also included some to achieve at home. This was to be a period of intense rehab with daily, weekly and long-term goals. One result of all of this activity was that Helen was more alert in the evening when I went to visit.

Other than her mother, brother and sister she had virtually no visitors during this period of rehab which she found very difficult. It was as though nobody else was interested in her apart from her family. In fact, she had very few visitors at all during her time in hospital or even when she was discharged. She learned that many assumed that others were visiting or that she only wanted family or that her rehab programme was so full that there was no room for visiting. We were quoted years ago that to 'assume' was to "make an ASS of U and ME". A good lesson to be learned. We later discovered that many had been informed from one source that she did not want any visitors which was far from the truth.

Wednesday 2nd May 2012

Psalms118:29 *"Give thanks to the Lord, for He is good; His love endures forever."*

Helen's major focus was on her balance and stability and she also worked on her concentration. Not only was the rehab working on improving these areas, but it was also looking at strategies to help her when 'normal faculties' do not work as well as before.

Helen looked forward to Fridays most of all. Not only did she come home in the afternoon for the weekend, but she had some sessions she enjoyed the most. The day started with a normal hospital breakfast as a 'keep you going' before she went to the Rehab kitchen for the breakfast club. This was where one of the OT's supervised a small number of the 'better' patients in preparing and eating their own breakfast. This often included various cooked items along with toast and of course more tea. This was highly enjoyable and was a bit like the TV program 'Ready, Steady Cook' as they never quite knew what they were going to have to cook with (or was that part of the exercise?) or whether they were all going to be there.

Friday was also the day for gardening club which Helen had signed up for. Within the RBH grounds there were small internal spaces down to the ground level which had been developed in various ways as they were off different wards. One of the spaces off the Rehab Physio rooms had been developed into a garden by an ex-patient who came in weekly to run the gardening club for the patients. The time involved various planting out and planning exercises. There was a small-green house and several raised beds with a variety of vegetables and various flowers and this area really put the other internal spaces to shame. Helen particularly enjoyed the opportunity to do something normal which did not have a report at the end or someone ticking off her achievements against a goals sheet.

The weekend was about ensuring that Helen could get herself around the village without getting lost, although she did not know that was the aim. We went out several times and I made her lead and decide where to go. She had to cross the roads safely and get home after she had been led a different way by me. Other trips included going round the shops in the village in a different order to usual and using the cut-through paths to bring us out in different places. She passed these 'little tests' with flying colours and then, on our second walk asked me if I was trying to get her lost, as if I would? There were other tasks for the weekend, but as usual the time flew by and it was soon time for her to get back to the RBH.

Monday 7th May

Psalms 119:57 *"You are my portion O Lord; I have promised to obey your words"* - We do need to know God as our 'portion' and our supply.

This week was once again set to be a busy one for Helen, and she was also to have a meeting to get the results of her assessment. The meeting was on Tuesday afternoon and Helens results were compared to what is considered 'normal' for her age group. The question is always what is 'normal'? What amazed everyone was how normal many of the results were when, one considers how bad the prognosis could have been. I will go through the results as they were given in the various areas.

1. *Processing.* Helen later said she felt like she was a computer that had been rebooted, and sometimes she has felt like a quad core processor which has one of the cores no longer functioning. Certainly her speed of processing had mild impairment and this was the cause of her fatigue. This would improve over time, but the question was how much? She would need to pace herself with some tasks and she had some difficulty holding on to multiple ideas.

2. *Concentration.* Helen's basic focus was fine, but her maintenance of concentration was affected by fatigue and her maximum period of concentration was about 45 minutes. She was able to remember sequences of information, but again this dropped off as fatigue increased. She was aware, however,

of her deficiencies and discussed how she can use lists to help her remember information. She did have difficulty cutting out background noise and distractions.
3. *Memory.* She had really good story recall, remembering about 95% immediately, with detail being lost over time. However, she was good at attempting to fill in the gaps herself. New learning was going to take time and we would often have to allow her to make her own notes and would have to give information at an appropriate time. She struggled with remembering linked words which was an executive function issue. Helen seemed to be very good at visualising what she needed to remember.
4. *Visual Spatial.* This was all about how Helen perceived things. She had a good idea how her life was structured and she had no perception issues, but she would need to look at how she structured her life from this point forward and how she used space to take stock to move forward. Helen seemed to have good self - awareness of what her difficulties were and what she needed to do to compensate for them.

She would need to allow more time to do tasks and would need to improve her planning significantly, allowing time to check her plan as she progressed. Her family would initially have to check that she was doing something safely and to take care especially where there was background noise.

Helen was referred to the Community Psychologist for help once she came home. The time it took to get this in place is another story

Wednesday 9th May

Psalms 119:89 - 90 *"Your word, Lord, is eternal; it stands firm in the heavens. Your faithfulness continues through all generations; You, established the earth, and it endures."*

God continues to be faithful in His healing of Helen and His undertaking for us all.

Wednesday involved a trip to Tesco Express to buy the food for Helen's cooking the next day. The OT tried to get her lost on the way back, but she had become wise to their tricks and was able to pre-empt what they were up to. She was going to be asked to cook a meal for one but in reality that was not what she would be doing at home. The OTs were not used to bulk cooking or just cooking with what was in the cupboard. Helen ended up teaching the OT quite a lot about home cooking for a family and how to make things go further. At the end of the cooking session there was enough food left for her to be able to share some with others on the ward. They all commented that this was better than the general hospital cooking. Some even asked her if she was prepared to start up her own cooking service, after the meal they had enjoyed and the breakfast club. However she found that the planning was the real issue. Whilst she could cook 'short term', it was the planning for the event which was a real problem as well as working out on what day she had to do things.

Helen had a timetable for the week but she found remembering what to do on what day difficult. In the end the only way she could remember was by constantly referring to the board in the ward and writing out her timetable several times for herself. Of course the timetable changed each week and so when she had just mastered one week it would all change. Change is one thing that someone with an acquired brain injury struggles with as well as adapting to that change, but then I suppose that was what they were wanting to achieve for Helen so that she did not become stuck in a routine.

Helen's case conference to discuss going home was scheduled for the next week. We had more to pack into the weekend at home because they wanted to know how she was coping with domestic duties as well as her own personal difficulties.

Chapter 23
Almost there
(Monday 16th May)

James 1:5 *"If any of you lacks wisdom, he should ask God who gives generously to all without finding fault."*

Helen had a packed timetable this week with many sessions every day. I had the opportunity to join her for the second part of a physio session and we had a discussion at the end about her balance. They said that her balance was as good as it would get in hospital and that now she needed to be walking greater distances, and for longer periods than she could while in hospital with hour-long sessions.

Tuesday was Helen's case conference to completely review where Helen had come from and what the long-term prognosis would be. All the respective parties had an input and they wanted Helen to come home on the morning of the Thursday before half-term. We had sowed the idea of half-term as this would allow all of us to be at home together for a week before Helen would be left on her own. They wanted her to go home on Thursday as the hospital wanted to move a new person onto the ward before the weekend. This, however, would not really work for us as someone would have needed to be at home with Helen for those two days and I had already taken quite a bit of time off from school, and expected to need more time over the next few months. All parties were amazed at Helen's progress considering the severity of the bleed and the potential brain damage that should have occurred from her lying for about 8 hours on the floor at home. They did say that her balance would improve, but they could not say how much, or how or when the fatigue would drop off although, they said that most people see the fatigue end within two years. The rest of the week was spent doing the usual rehab tasks and several sessions of the gardening club as there was quite a bit of preparation to do to the flower beds before they were to be planted out.

Again, Helen was allowed to go home for the weekend and do all her usual business and domestic tasks. She also wanted to make lots of cakes to take back into the hospital for her final week.

Chapter 24
The final week in the RBH
(Monday 23rd May 2012)

This was to be Helen's final week in the RBH. She was to have a final set of sessions and she was given vast amounts of information to take home. The one thing the staff focused on was scheduling and planning so that Helen could look ahead and plan her weeks. This was important, but it took her quite a while once she was home to grasp the concept and fully put it into practice.

On Thursday I took the cakes in for all the staff. They were so delighted and they wanted to put in an order for weekly cakes. They had been very good to Helen and she had made significant progress, so on the Friday she was duly discharged. However, we came to ask ourselves, just how long does it take to get medicine from the pharmacy? They knew she was leaving and yet at 3.00pm the drugs had not even been signed for by a doctor. Some things about hospitals are so frustrating. We eventually got away by 4.15pm. The boys came to the hospital so that as a family we could have closure on that aspect of Helen's recovery.

Chapter 25
HOME
(Friday 27th May 2012)

It was great to be home knowing that on Sunday we would not have to take Helen back to the hospital. We all slept well that night and had a relaxing few days. The first week was spent trying to get back to as normal a life as possible although we were all very aware that we needed to get Helen into a home routine and able to look after herself. So it was 'chart creation city' to the fore so that the essential parts of her life were organised and so that she had all the coping strategies in place. We tried to prepare all the things she would need when the boys and I went back to school the following week. The weather was not good and the week became wetter as the days went on and the river at the bottom of the village was getting higher and higher.

We did manage some walks in the area and Helen came to Asda with me, but at this stage it was obvious that she could not cope on her own with a supermarket and certainly not one that had been rearranged since her last visit. Helen spent most of the time hanging onto the trolley whilst I did all the running around. She could not walk and scan the shelves at the same time and this was to be an ongoing issue.

Helen was determined to get back to driving at some point and I managed to get hold of someone from the Regional Driving Assessment Centre (RDAC) who were really helpful in explaining the situation and told they us how to get Helen back in a car at the appropriate point of her recovery. She was already starting to react to my driving and her right foot was going for the brake on a number of occasions. So after some discussion we decided to book Helen for a driving assessment for the end of August. We discovered that if someone is in hospital for more than a month then you should have your driving re-assessed, but it is not necessary to surrender a driving licence to DVLA if an assessment has been booked, you just have to assure them that you will not drive before the assessment.

Over the last weekend of half-term it had rained continually and the river rose even higher and, by Monday morning, the road at the bottom of the village was only just passable in the middle. I duly managed to make it to school and Timothy and Stephen went on the coach as usual. I rang Helen at 8.00am to tell her I had arrived at school however she did not reply and the phone just rang and rang. So I assumed she was in the bathroom. I rang again fifteen minutes later, but still there was no reply. So I duly did my tutor group and then tried again. I guess you can sense what I was feeling by now. The first day we leave Helen alone… I also tried ringing the neighbours, but to no avail. I had no alternative but to make a "quick" trip home to see if Helen was ok. I quickly chatted with my line manager, arranged cover and off I set.

The road into Mortimer was now impassable, so I had to turn around and find another route, via central Reading and a less flooded road. Radio Berkshire was brilliant as their road reports were giving all the blocked and passable roads. I duly reached home over an hour later to find Helen happily eating a late breakfast and learned that all the telephones in the village were out due to flooding. I had a quick cuppa, de-stress and then went back to work relieved. At the end of the day my line manager and I had a good laugh about it and school were very understanding.

So what about our children in all of this? Well, just before the end of their school year we received notification that they were both to receive a prize at school for 'academic progress under adverse situations'. They had been recommended for the prize by over seven teachers as well as the head teacher. The evening they received that prize we were so proud. This was a clear indication that God had His hand on them through it all.

So after an exciting start, we gradually returned to normal.

Chapter 26
Things are not quite right

Towards the end of June, Helen went for an MRI at the RBH to check the blood vessels in her head and unbeknown to us the rehab consultant was not completely happy with what he saw and so referred Helen to the Neuro team at the JR. They called her for an MRI in their machine which has higher definition. This took place on a Sunday afternoon when the JR seemed very empty. There was only a single receptionist in the CT department and no one else around, the place was a bit of a ghost town. The images were to be reviewed at the Neuro Department team meeting the next Monday.

Again, this team were not sure about what they saw and so they decided to do a high resolution CT scan with dye enhancing the blood vessels in her head. Thankfully they were happy with what they saw this time and so they sent her home with the message 'go and live the rest of your life'. At 5.00pm the same day, we had another call to say that at the team meeting, they were, in fact not happy and they wanted her to be very careful with her activities and they would call her back for further investigations later in the summer. Helen was not to do anything strenuous or to lift anything. Next morning we received a call to say that they wanted Helen in that day for an angiogram, a scan which looks specifically at the blood vessels of the brain, with the option to coil another aneurysm which they had found. So that evening we went back to the JR to admit Helen for the next day.

I was at the JR at the crack of dawn the next day having left the boys at home on their own. We were supposed to be in Worcester setting up for the Bible Week for which we were the administrators.

If you ever have to have a procedure like this, the consent forms are huge-A3 in size and several pages long. The surgeon went through all the risks involved. There was no trouble in remembering the date as it was Helen's birthday. She was taken down for the procedure which was to be conducted under a general anaesthetic. I then sat down at my minibook to write a set of instructions on how to set up the Bible Week for those who were suddenly faced with having to do our jobs themselves.

The procedure took several hours and afterwards the consultant came to see me to tell me how well it had gone and that Helen now had £10,000 of coils in her head and that it was his birthday present to her. She came round quickly, but she had to remain in hospital until the Friday.

When we cane to leave one of the nurses came to me and said that she needed some paperwork completed before we left, I duly went with her and there were forms for our private health care claim she needed me to complete. I questioned why we were to complete these as we were NHS patients. "Oh" she said, "we thought you were private patients". No wonder Helen had been treated so well with her own room, nurse and excellent food.

We did make it to the Bible Week on the Sunday and we also managed to get away for a week's holiday in our caravan.

Chapter 27
So you want to drive (again)

Anyone who has been in hospital for a month or more is not allowed to drive without an assessment of their capability to drive (these were the rules in 2012). These are carried out at regional assessment centres. There are two ways to do this. First is to tell the DVLA that you wish to drive again (there is up to a three month delay whilst they make all the arrangements and they insist you submit your driving licence). They arrange the test, and you need to have a special provisional single day licence for this. The results are sent to them (you wait up to three more months) and then you get the results.

The other way is for you to arrange and pay for the assessment yourself and if you pass you can drive from that moment and the assessment report is yours to send to DVLA and your insurance company.

Helen went for the assessment. There are two components, an interview with the assessor and an OT, and then you go out on the road. You have to use one of their cars and the driving session is just under an hour and a half with three sections, each more involved than the last. At the end of the session we received the feedback, that 'there is no cognitive reason why Helen cannot drive', but she might benefit from some refresher sessions if she needed to drive on the motorway right away. God is so good. He had brought such healing.

The next day Helen was to meet the rehab consultant to follow up her progress over the last few months. This took place at the local community hospital and we did not know that he was watching our arrival and observing Helen walking across the carpark. When we went in to see him, he was blown away with her progress and stated that "she stood more chance of winning the lottery on a weekly ticket every week for a year, than having the recovery he saw before him." He was truly amazed. He went through all that Helen was doing and saw that she had passed her driving assessment. It was a truly remarkable set of results.

Chapter 28
Finally

Where we are now and what happened next is another story in itself. What happened when Helen returned to work is all documented but must remain so for the time being.

What happened to the boys and how they survived a very traumatic period is for them to tell at some stage, but thrive they did and Timothy is now a qualified doctor at a London hospital and Stephen is a mechanical engineer, and expert gear cutter. How they got there is another story.

Sufficient to say that many families, who go through what we went through see breakdowns, children becoming school refusers or dropping out completely and entering the drug culture. The fact that none of this happened is entirely due to the grace and provision of God, and our faith and trust in Him.

What happened to Helen during those 8 hours on the floor is the only thing she can remember clearly from a six-week gap in her memory. What she saw and who she met, will have to be another book.

SO, it would be wrong not to end without thanking all our family and friends who supported and prayed for us through that difficult time and who continue to do so. To those who provided us with a meal every day for sixteen weeks and to the person who so brilliantly coordinated those meals. Also to those across the world who we will never meet this side of glory but who simply prayed, you reward awaits you.

And to the God, who we serve, who bought our salvation through the death and resurrection of Jesus and who needs to get all the glory for the outcome you have read in these pages. If you do not know Him personally, can I encourage you to seek Him out.

Printed in Great Britain
by Amazon